Religious Reality

By

A.E.J. Rawlinson

Preface

1918

By the Bishop of Lichfield

This is a book which is wanted. Thoughtful men, in every class, are not afraid of theology, i.e. of a reasoned account of their religion, but they want a theology which can be stated without conventions and technicalities; they do not at all care for a religion which pretends to do away with all mystery, but they are glad to be assured of the essential reasonableness of the Christian Faith; they do not expect a ready-made solution of the problem of evil, but they wish to see it honestly faced; above all, they want to know how Christian truth bears on the real problems of life; the best of them are not at all afraid of a religion which makes big demands on them, but they know well enough the difficulty of responding to those claims, and their greatest need of all is to find and to use that life and power, coming from a living Person, without which our best aspirations must fail and our highest ideals remain unrealized.

These needs seem to me to be satisfactorily and happily met in the following pages. My friend and chaplain, Mr. Bawlinson, has had good means of knowing what men are and what they want. He has had to do with the undergraduate, with officers and men in the Army, and with the ordinary civilian in parish life. He has been able to see the nature and needs of our British manhood at different angles, and he is the sort of man with whom men are not afraid to talk. He has had good opportunity of diagnosing the situation, and this book shows his skill in dealing with it.

I do not find myself in agreement with everything in these pages, but when I am conscious of difference of view, I am no less grateful for the stimulus to thought. I am specially thankful that the writer has been so courageous in tackling the most difficult subjects.

I know that the author's one desire is to help men to be more real in their religion. I share his hope, and I believe that this book will do much to accomplish it.

Author's Preface This book has grown out of the writer's experience in preparing men and officers in military hospitals for Confirmation. It represents, in a considerably expanded but—as it is hoped—still simple form, the kind of things which he would have wished to say to them, and to others with whom he was brought into contact, if he had had more time and opportunity than was usually afforded him. It seemed necessary to write the book, because there did not appear to be in existence any reasonably short book on similar lines which covered the ground of Christian faith and practice as a whole, and which approached the subject from the point of view which seems to the writer to be the most real.

The writer is consciously indebted in the first chapter to the discussion of our Lord's teaching and character in Dr. T. B. Glover's fascinating book, The Jesus of History. It is possible that there are other and unconscious obligations which have been overlooked. Here and there acknowledgment is made in footnotes, and an occasional phrase, "lifted" from some other writer, has been placed in inverted commas.

In Chapter VIII. of Part I. the author has echoed the thought, and to a certain extent the wording, of parts of his own essay on "The Principle of Authority" in Foundations.

For help in the correction of the proofs, and for criticisms and suggestions which have led to numerous modifications and improvements in matters of detail, the thanks of the writer are due to various friends, and more particularly to his brother, Lieutenant A. C. Rawlinson, of the Queen's Own Oxfordshire Hussars; to the Rev. Austin Thompson, Vicar of S. Peter's, Eaton Square; and to the Rev. Leonard Hodgson, Vice-Principal of S. Edmund Hall, Oxford.

November, 1917.

Introduction

Vital religion begins for a man when lie first discovers the reality of the living GOD. Most men indeed profess a belief in GOD, a vague acknowledgment of the existence of "One above": but the belief counts for little in their lives.

GOD, if He exists at all, must obviously be important: and it is conceivable that He prefers the dogmatic atheism of a man here and a man there, or the serious agnosticism of a slightly larger number, to the practical indifference of the majority. "There are two attitudes, and only two, which are worthy of a serious man: to serve GOD with his whole heart, because he knows Him; or to seek GOD with his whole heart, because he knows Him not."

The ordinary Englishman is in most cases nominally a Christian. As a rule he has been admitted in infancy by baptism into the Christian Church. But he is ignorant of the implications of his baptism, and indifferent to the claims of a religion which he fails to understand. These pages are written with the object of explaining what, in the writer's judgment, the faith and practice of the Christian Church really is.

Part I

The Theory of the Christian Religion

Chapter I

the Man Christ Jesus

It is best to begin with a study of the teaching and character of Christ. Scholars for about a hundred years have been studying the Gospels historically, "like any other books." It is now reasonably certain that the first three Gospels–those which we know as the Gospels according to S. Matthew, S. Mark, and S. Luke–though not, of course, infallible or accurate in their every detail, reflect nevertheless in a general way a trustworthy portrait of Jesus as He actually lived. The sayings ascribed to Christ in their pages bear the marks of originality. The outline of the events which they describe may be taken as being in rough correspondence with the facts. The Gospels as a whole represent pretty faithfully the impression made by the life and character of Jesus upon the minds and memories of those who knew Him best.

We are very apt to regard the Gospels conventionally. An inherited orthodoxy which has made peace with the world takes them for granted as "a tale of little meaning, though the words are strong." An impatient reaction from orthodoxy sets them aside as incomprehensible or unimportant. It is worth while making the effort to empty our minds of prejudice, and to allow the Gospels to tell their own tale. We shall find that they bring us face to face with a Portrait of surprising freshness and power.

It is the portrait of One who spent the first thirty years of His life in an obscure Galilaean village, and who in early manhood worked as a carpenter in a village shop. He first came forward in public in connexion with a religious revival initiated by John the Baptist. He was baptized in the Jordan. What His baptism meant to Him is symbolized by the account of a vision which He saw, and a Voice which designated Him as Son of

GOD. He became conscious of a religious mission, and was at first tempted to interpret His mission in an unworthy way, to seek to promote spiritual ends by temporal compromises, or to impress men's minds by an appeal to mystery or miracle. He rejected the temptation, and proclaimed simply GOD and His Kingdom. He is said to have healed the sick and to have wrought other "signs and mighty works": but He set no great store by these things, and did not wish to be known primarily as a wonder-worker. He lived the life of an itinerating Teacher, declaring to any who cared to listen the things concerning the Kingdom of GOD. At times He was popular and attracted crowds: but He cared little for popularity, wrapped up His teaching in parables, and repelled by His "hard sayings" all but a minority of earnest souls. He gave offence to the conventionalists and the religiously orthodox by the freedom with which He criticized established beliefs and usages, by His championship of social outcasts, and by His association with persons of disreputable life. Unlike John the Baptist, He was neither a teetotaller nor a puritan. He was not a rigid Sabbatarian. He despised humbug, hypocrisy, and cant: and He hated meanness and cruelty. He could be stern with a terrible sternness. His gaze pierced through all disguises, and He understood the things that are in the heart of man. He saw things naked. He has been called "the great Son of Fact." He was never under any illusions.

He faced the hostility of public opinion with unflinching courage. He expected to be crucified, and crucified He was. He warned those who followed Him to expect a similar fate. He claimed from men an allegiance that should be absolute: the ties of home and kindred, of wealth or position in the world, were to be held of no account: anything which stood in the way of entire discipleship to Himself, however compelling its immediate claim, was to be sacrificed without hesitation for His sake. He saw nothing inconsistent between this concentration of men's allegiance upon His own person, and His insistence upon GOD as the one great Reality that mattered.

The motive of His whole life was consecration to the will of GOD. He was rich towards GOD, where other men are poor. The words were true of Him, as of no one else, "I have set GOD always before me." His mission among men He fulfilled as a work which His Father had given Him to do. "Lo, I come to do Thy will, O GOD." He loved men, and went about doing good, because He knew that GOD loved men, and meant well by them, and desired good for them, and not evil. He was pitiful, because GOD is pitiful. He hated evil, because GOD hates it. He loved purity, because GOD is pure.

He delighted in friendships both with men and women: but you could not imagine anything unclean in His friendships. He was not married, but He looked upon marriage as an utterly pure and holy thing, taught that a man should leave father and mother and cleave unto his wife so that they twain should be one flesh, and recognized no possibility of divorce except—and even this is not quite certain—on the ground of marital unfaithfulness. He had one and the same standard of purity for men and women.

He loved children, the birds and the flowers, the life of the open air: but He was equally at home in the life of the town. He went out to dinner with anybody who asked Him: He rejoiced in the simple hilarity of a wedding feast. He was a believer in fellowship, and in human brotherhood. He was everybody's friend, and looked upon no one as beyond the pale. He loved sinners and welcomed them, without in the least condoning what was wrong. He looked upon the open and acknowledged sinner as a more hopeful person from the religious point of view than the person who was self-satisfied and smug. He said that He came to seek and to save those who knew themselves to be lost.

He chose twelve men to be in an especial sense His disciples—learners in His school. To them He sought to reveal something of His deeper mind. He tried to make them understand that true royalty consists in service; that if a man would be spiritually great he should choose for himself the lowest room, and become the servant of all; that the privilege of sitting on His right hand and on His left in His Kingdom was reserved for those for whom it was prepared by His Father; the important thing was whether a man was prepared to drink His cup of suffering, and be baptized with His baptism of blood. But He did speak of Himself as King, He accepted the designation of Himself as the Christ of GOD, and spoke strange words about His coming upon the clouds of heaven to judgment. He held that by their relation to Himself and to His ideals the lives of all men should be tested, and the verdict passed upon their deeds. For making these and similar claims He was convicted of blasphemy and put to death.

His disciples failed to understand Him. The Gospels are full of the contrast between their minds and His. Of the chosen Twelve who, as He said, had continued with Him in His trials and to whom He promised that they should eat and drink at His table in His Kingdom, and sit on thrones judging the twelve tribes of Israel, one betrayed and one denied Him when the time of crisis came, and the rest forsook Him and fled. The fact that their faith and loyalty were subsequently re- established–that the execution which took place on Calvary was not the complete and summary ending of the whole Christian movement–that, in the days that followed, the recreant disciples became the confident Apostles, requires for its explanation the assertion in some form of the truth of the Resurrection.

With regard to the precise form which the Resurrection took there may be room for differences of opinion: the accounts of the risen Jesus in the various Gospel records cannot be completely harmonized, and the story may here and there have been modified in the telling. The fact remains that apart from the assumption as a matter of historical truth that Jesus was veritably alive from the dead, and that He showed Himself alive to His disciples by evidences which were adequate to carry conviction to their incredulous minds, the origins of historical Christianity cannot really be explained.

In the Gospel according to S. John it is stated that the crowds said of Jesus, "This is of a truth that Prophet that should come into the world": and so much, at the least, the average

Englishman is ready to admit: for to call Jesus Christ a Prophet—even to call Him the supreme Prophet—is to claim for Him no more than a good Mohammedan claims for Mohammed.

The word "prophet" in itself means one who speaks on behalf of another: and a prophet is defined to be a spokesman on behalf of GOD. He is essentially a man with a message. In so far as he is a true prophet he is one who by an imperious inner necessity is constrained to declare to his fellows a word which has come to him from the Lord. And the prophet's word is urgent: it brooks no delay. It is impatient of conventionalisms and shams. It breaks through the established order of things in matters both social and religious. It is dynamic, vivid, revolutionary. It goes to the root of things, with a startling directness, a kind of explosive force. It disturbs and shatters the customary placidities of men's lives. It forces them to face spiritual realities, to look the truth in the face.

All this is true in a pre-eminent degree of the words of Christ. There is a force and directness, an energy and intensity about His teaching, which is without parallel in the history of the world. It might have been thought impossible for His utterances, in any age or under any circumstances, to become conventionalized: but the miracle has been achieved. Christianity is to the average Englishman an established convention and nothing more.

"Blessed are the poor in spirit," said Jesus: but we say rather, "Blessed are the rich in substance."

"Blessed are they that mourn": but that is not the general opinion.

"Blessed are the meek, for they shall inherit the earth"—but who amongst us really believes it?

"Blessed are they that hunger and thirst after righteousness: for they shall be filled."

"Blessed are the merciful: for they shall obtain mercy": but to-day a more popular maxim is, "Be not merciful unto them that offend of malicious wickedness."

"Blessed are the pure in heart"—and how many of us are that?

"Blessed are the peace-makers": but in a time of war they are not very favourably regarded.

"Blessed are they that are persecuted for righteousness' sake"–is that your ambition, or mine?

"Ye are the salt of the earth" and "the light of the world"– then the earth, it is to be feared, is a somewhat insipid place, and its light comparable to darkness visible. "If any man will come after Me, let him take up his Cross, and follow Me": but most of us make it a tacit condition of our Christianity that we shall not be crucified.

Is it not true that we habitually refuse to take seriously His teaching about man; that we water down His paradoxes and conventionalize His sayings; that we blunt the sharpness of His precepts, and shirk the tremendous sternness of His demands?

And does His teaching about GOD fare any better? GOD was to Jesus Christ the one Reality that mattered; is that in any serious sense true of us? GOD, He taught, cares for the sparrows, numbers the hairs of our heads, sees in secret, and reads our inmost hearts. GOD knows all about us, loves us individually, thinks out our life in all its relations, and makes provision accordingly. There is nothing which He cannot or will not do for His children.

He is near and not far off: He is also on the throne of all things– the Universe is in our Father's hand, and His will directs it. "O ye of little faith, wherefore did ye doubt?" Fear, on the ground that things are stormy, is a thing Christ simply cannot understand.

GOD, moreover, is loving and generous, royal and bounteous: forgiving sinners: sending His rain with Divine impartiality upon the just and the unjust alike. "His flowers are just as beautiful in the bad man's garden." He loves even His enemies, for He is equally the Father of all.

And man is made for GOD, and belongs to GOD. GOD and man need one another: all that is requisite is that they should find one another: and that is the Good News. The discovery of GOD is the Pearl of great price, a Treasure worth the sacrifice of everything else: the experience of a life-time, and a life-time's acquisitions, apart from GOD, are not worth anything at all.

We who call ourselves Christians, do we seriously believe these things? Do we really share Christ's outlook upon GOD, or His hope for man? Is our view of life centred in GOD, as was His? Or do His words of reproach fit us, as they fitted S. Peter—"You think like a man, and not like GOD"?

"The way to faith in GOD, and to love for man," it has been said, "is to come nearer to the living Jesus." If we would learn Christ's great prophecy about man and GOD, we must read the Gospels over again, with awakened eyes. We must take seriously the man Christ Jesus. We must hear the words of His prophecy, and face honestly the challenge of His sayings. We must confront the central Figure of the Gospels in all its tremendous realism, watering down nothing, explaining nothing away; "wrestling with Jesus of Nazareth as Jacob wrestled with the angel, and refusing to let Him go except He bless us." In the end He does bless those who wrestle with Him, and we shall not in the end be able to stop short of confessing Him as GOD.

For the message of the Gospel story is ultimately not even the teaching of Christ: it is Christ Himself. He, alone among the world's teachers, perfectly practised what He preached, and embodied what He taught. And therefore the truth of GOD and the ideal for man in Him are one. In Him we see man as he ought to be, man as he is meant to be. And because we instinctively judge that the highest human nature is divine, and because also we feel that GOD Himself would be most divine and worshipful if we could conceive of Him as entering in and sharing our human experience and revealing Himself as man, those who have reflected most deeply about the matter have commonly been led to believe that so indeed it is. They have felt that in Jesus Christ man, as the mirror and the Son of GOD, reflects the Father's glory. They have felt that in Jesus Christ GOD, the Eternal Source of all things, has expressed and revealed Himself in a human life: that GOD has spoken a Word, a Word which is the expression of Himself: and that the Word is Christ. "Have I been so long time with you, and yet hast thou not known Me, Philip? He that hath seen Me, hath seen the Father." For there is, in truth, something in Jesus of Nazareth which compels our worship. And if we will take seriously the human Jesus we shall discover in the end Deity revealed in manhood, and we shall worship Him in whom we have believed.

But that, of course, is dogma: in other words, it is the deliberate judgment of Christian faith. It is the expression, as a truth for the mind, of the value which a soul which is spiritually awake comes to set upon Jesus because it cannot do otherwise. A judgment like that is the conclusion—it ought not to be taken as the starting-point—of faith. There are many, of course, who are willing to begin by assuming provisionally that it is true, upon the authority of others who bear witness to it: and that is not an unreasonable thing to do, provided a man afterwards verifies it in the experience of his own life. But belief in the divinity of Jesus is too tremendous a confession lightly to be taken for granted by mere half-believers of a casual creed. Convictions worth having must sooner or later be fought for: they must be won by the sweat of the brow. And if a man is not content permanently to defer to the authority of others, he ought not to begin by taking for granted the doctrine that Jesus is GOD. He ought to begin as the Apostles began, by taking seriously the Man Christ Jesus.

Chapter II

The Revelation of the Father

It was characteristic of the ancient Jews that they had a vital belief in the living GOD: and belief in GOD, and that of a far more real and definite kind than the modern Englishman's vague admission of the existence of a Supreme Being, was a thing which Jesus was able to take for granted in those to whom He spoke. GOD to the Jew was the GOD of Abraham, Isaac, and Jacob, holy and righteous, gracious and merciful: active and operative in the world, the Controller of events: having a purpose for Israel and for the world, which in the process of the world's history was being wrought out, and which would one day find complete and adequate fulfilment in the setting up of GOD'S Eternal Kingdom.

What Jesus did by His life and teaching was to deepen and intensify existing faith in GOD by the revelation of GOD as Father, and to revive and quicken the expectation of GOD'S Kingdom by the proclamation of its near approach. The application to GOD of the term "Father" was not new: but the revelation of what GOD'S Fatherhood meant in the personal life and faith of Jesus Himself as Son of God was something entirely new: while in Jesus' preaching of the Divine Kingdom there was a note of freshness and originality, and a spiritual assurance of certainty, which carried conviction of an entirely new kind to the minds and hearts of those who listened.

All the more overwhelming must have seemed to the disciples the disaster of their Master's crucifixion. It was not merely that the hopes which in their minds had gathered about His person were shattered: their very faith in GOD Himself, and in the goodness of GOD, was for the time being torn up by the roots. Nothing but an event as real and as objective as the Crucifixion itself could have reversed for them this impression of sheer catastrophe. The resurrection of Jesus, which was for them the wonder of wonders, not only restored to them their faith in Him as the Christ of GOD, now "declared to be the Son of

GOD with power by the resurrection from the dead"; it also relaid for them the foundations of faith in GOD and in His goodness and love upon a basis of certainty henceforth never to be shaken. "This is the message which we have heard of Him and declare unto you, that GOD is light, and in Him is no darkness at all."

Meanwhile what of Jesus Himself—this Christ, through their relationship to whom they had come by this new experience of the reality of GOD? In symbolical vision they saw Him ascend up into the heavens and vanish from bodily sight: in pictorial language they spoke of Him as seated at GOD'S right hand. They were assured nevertheless— and multitudes in many generations have echoed their conviction—that He was still in their midst unseen, their living Master and Lord. Instinctively they prayed to Him. Through Him they made their approach to the Father. He had transformed for them their world. He was the light of their lives. In Him was truth. He was their way to GOD.

All the great movement of Christian thought in the New Testament is concerned in one way or another with the working out of this experienced significance of Jesus. The maturest expression of what He meant to them is contained in the great reflective Gospel—an interpretation rather than a simple portrait of the historical Jesus— which is ascribed by tradition to S. John. The Christ of the Fourth Gospel is man, with all the attributes of most real and genuine manhood: but He is also more than man. He is the self-utterance—the Word—of GOD. He came forth from GOD, and went to GOD. He is the revelation of the Father, the expression of GOD'S nature and being "in the intelligible terms of a human life." To have seen Him is to have seen the Father, because He and the Father are one. He is the Way, the Truth, and the Life: the Bread that came down from heaven: the Fountain of living water: the Lamb of GOD, that taketh away the sin of the world.

Later Christian orthodoxy never got farther than this. All that the formal doctrine of the Incarnation—as expressed, for example, in such a formulary as the Athanasian Creed—can truly be said to amount to is just the double insistence that Christ is at once truly and completely man, and also truly and completely GOD. The paradox is left unreconciled—"yet He is not two, but one Christ." The Godhead is expressed in manhood: in the manhood we see GOD.

What does it mean to confess the Deity of Christ? It means just this: that we take the character of Christ as our clue to the character of GOD: that we interpret the life of Christ as an expression of the life of GOD: that we affirm the conviction, based upon deep and unshakable personal experience, that "GOD was in Christ reconciling the world unto Himself."

What is the real question, the most fundamental of questions, which arises when we seek to interpret the world we live in? Is it not just the question: What is the nature or character of the ultimate Power or Principle or Person upon which or upon whom the world depends? Is not every religion, every imagined deity, in one sense an altar to the unknown GOD? The venture of Christian faith consists in staking all upon the assumption, the hypothesis abundantly verified in the life's experience of such as make it, that the character of the unknown GOD is revealed in Christ: that the love of Christ is the expression of the love of GOD, the sufferings of Christ an expression of the suffering of GOD, the triumph of Christ an expression of the eternal victory of GOD over all the evil and wickedness which mars the wonder of His creation. If we were to look primarily at the life of Nature, we might be tempted to say that GOD was cruel. If we considered certain of the works of man, we might be tempted to conclude that GOD was devilish. Looking at Jesus we gain the assurance that GOD is Love. We behold "the light of the knowledge of the glory of GOD in the face of Jesus Christ," and we are satisfied.

And so we come to Jesus—the Prophet that is come into the world: and what we shall find, if we will suffer Him to work His work in us, is this. He will change our world for us, and will transform it. He will redeem our souls, so that there shall be in us a new birth, a new creation. He will show us the Father, and it

16

shall suffice us. He will set our feet on the road to Calvary, and we shall rejoice to be crucified with Him. He will convert us—He will turn our lives inside out, so that they shall have their centre in GOD, and no longer in ourselves. He will bestow on us the Spirit without measure, so that we shall be sons and daughters of the Highest. And we shall know that we are of GOD, even though the whole world lieth in wickedness. And we shall know that the Son of GOD is come, and that He hath given us an understanding, that we may know Him that is true, and that we are in Him that is true, even in His Son Jesus Christ.

Chapter III - The Fellowship of the SpiritTo know GOD and to find Him revealed in Jesus Christ is not enough. To have set before one in the human life of Jesus an ideal of character, a pattern of perfect manhood for imitation, if the message of the Gospel were regarded as stopping short at that point, could only be discouraging to men conscious of moral weakness, of spiritual impotence and incapacity. It is probable that one of the reasons why the plain man to-day is so very apt to regard Christianity as consisting in the profession of a standard of ideal morality to which he knows himself to be personally incapable of attaining, and which those who do profess it fail conspicuously to practise, is to be found in the entire absence from his mind and outlook of any conception of the Holy Spirit, or any belief in the availability of the Spirit as a source of transforming energy and power in the lives of men.

As a matter of fact, the doctrine of the Holy Spirit is of absolutely vital importance in the Christian scheme: and like all the great Christian doctrines, it has its basis in the realities of living experience. The opening chapters of the Acts of the Apostles set before us the picture of the earliest disciples, assured and no longer doubtful of the reality of the Resurrection, waiting in Jerusalem for a promised endowment of "power from on high." And the story of Pentecost is the record of the fulfilment of "the promise of the Father."

We are making a mistake if we fix our attention primarily upon the outward symbols of wind and fire, or confuse our minds with the perplexities which are suggested by the references to "speaking with tongues." These things—however wonderful to the men of the Apostolic generation—are in themselves only examples of the psychological abnormalities which not infrequently accompany religious revivals. They are, as it were, the foam on the crest of the wave: evidences upon the surface of profounder forces astir in the deeper levels of personality. The disciples felt themselves taken hold of and transformed. Henceforth they were new men. "GOD had sent into their hearts through Jesus Christ a Power not of this world: only such a power could achieve what history assures us was achieved by those early Christians. By its compelling influence they found themselves welded together into a religious and social community, a fellowship of faith and hope and love, the true Israel, the Church of the living GOD. Enabled to become daily more and more like Jesus, they developed an ever fuller comprehension of His unique significance: and so they went about carrying on the work and teaching which He had begun on earth, certain that He was with them and energizing in them. They healed the sick in mind and body, they convinced Jewish and Pagan consciences of sin and its forgiveness, they created a new morality, and established a new hope: life and immortality were brought to light. And then, as need arose, they were inspired to write those books of the New Testament, in which their wonderful experience of GOD at work in them remains enshrined, the norm and standard of Christian faith and practice for all time. The Power which enabled them to do all this they called the Holy Spirit." [1]

To be "filled with the Spirit," to be "endued with power from on high," to be made free by the Spirit, so as to be free indeed— released from the tyranny of a dead past, from bondage to law and literalism, from the power of sin and of evil habit—and to be brought forth into the glorious liberty of the sons of GOD: this was a very vital and essential part of what Christianity meant in the experience of those first disciples. The new morality of the

---

[1] The Holy Spirit, by R. G. Parsons, in The Meaning of the Creed. (S.P.C.K., 1917)

Gospel, the new righteousness which was to exceed the righteousness of Pharisees and Scribes, was a thing as widely removed as possible from painful conformity to the letter of an external code: it was a fruit—a spontaneous outcome—of the Spirit. S. Paul has described for us the fruits of the Spirit as he had seen them manifested in the lives of men—"love, joy, peace, long-suffering, kindness, goodness, faithfulness, meekness, self-control": they are the essential lineaments of the character of Christ: they are summed up in the thirteenth chapter of I Corinthians in S. Paul's great hymn to Charity or Love, which itself reads like yet another portrait of the Christ. A Christianity which through the Spirit brought forth such fruits was true to type. The Spirit, in short, reproduced in men the life of filial relationship towards GOD: He is described as the Spirit of adoption, whereby men are enabled to cry Abba, Father.

The Holy Spirit, moreover, is a Spirit of insight and interpretation, quickening men's faculties, enlightening their minds, enabling them to see, and to understand. He brings to remembrance the things of Christ and unfolds their significance: under His inspiration Christian preaching was developed, and a Christian doctrine about Christ and about GOD. In confident reliance upon His advocacy and His support the Apostles were made bold to confront in the name of Jesus a hostile world. Is it any wonder that in the eyes of their contemporaries they appeared as men possessed, as men made drunk with the new wine of some strange ecstasy, or mad with the fervour of some inexplicable exaltation? Yet the Spirit did not normally issue in ecstasy. It is not the way of GOD to over-ride men's reason, or to place their individual personalities in abeyance. The operation of the Spirit is to be seen rather—apart from His work in the gradual purification and deepening of character and motive, the bringing to birth and development in men's souls of the "new man" who is "Christ in them, the hope of glory"—in the intensification of men's normal faculties and gifts, and the direction of their exercise into channels profitable to the well-being of the community. For the Holy Spirit is the Spirit of brotherhood: and His gifts are bestowed "for the fitting of GOD'S people for the work of mutual service": they are for the upbuilding of the Body of Christ. The real miracle of the Christian life is simply the Christian life itself: and that a man should love his neighbour as himself is at least as wonderful as that he should speak with tongues.

Reflecting upon the experience which had come to them, Christian men came to see that the Holy Spirit, who was the Spirit of the Father and the Son, was Divine, even as Jesus was Divine. In this strange Power which had transformed their lives they discovered GOD, energizing and operative in their hearts. Instinctively they worshipped and glorified the Spirit as the Lord, the Giver of Life. Those who have entered upon any genuine measure of Christian experience are not prepared to say that they were wrong.

The Christian life depends upon the Spirit, now as then. Only in the power of the Holy Spirit is Christianity possible, and no one ever yet made any real advance in personal religion except in dependence upon an enabling energy of which the source was not in himself. "It is the Spirit that maketh alive." "The Spirit helpeth our infirmities." "I know that in myself, that is, in my flesh, dwelleth no good thing." "If ye, being evil, know how to give good gifts unto your children, how much more shall your heavenly Father give the Holy Spirit to them that ask Him." It is because of our lack of any living or effectual belief in the Holy Spirit, and because of our consequent failure to seek His inspiration and to submit ourselves to His influence, that the Christianity of men to-day is often so barren and so poor a thing; and the corporate life of Christendom languishes for the same reason. The Church is meant to be a fellowship, a brotherhood: the most real and living brotherhood on earth. Men find to-day the realization of brotherhood in a regiment: they find it in a school or in a club: in a Trade Union: or in such an organization as the Workers' Educational Association. They fail to find it in the Church of Christ.

The Church can never be a brotherhood save in the Holy Spirit: for Christianity is essentially and before all things a religion of the Spirit, and the external organization and institutions of the Church, apart from "His vivifying breath, are a mere empty shell. Where there is no vision the people perish: and it is only under the inspiration of the Spirit that men see visions and dream dreams. Come from the four winds, O Breath, and breathe upon these dry bones of our modern churchmanship, that we may live: and so at last shall we stand upright on our feet, an exceeding great army, and go forth conquering and to conquer in the train of the victorious Christ."

Chapter IV

The Holy Trinity

God, as Christianity reveals Him, is no cold or remote Being, no abstract Principle-of-All-Things, reposing aloof and impersonal in the stillness of an eternal calm. He is rather the boundless energy of an eternal Life—"no motionless eternity of perfection, but an overflowing vitality, an inexhaustible fecundity, the everlasting well-spring of all existence." He is the eternal Creator of all things; not indeed in any sense which commits us to a literal acceptance of the mythology of Genesis, but in the sense that the created universe has its origin in His holy and righteous will, and that upon Him all things depend. "In affirming that the world was made by GOD, we do not affirm that it was ready-made from the beginning." The work of creation is still going on. GOD is eternally making all things new.

The nature of GOD, in so far as the mind and affections of man are capable of knowing Him and entering into relationships with Him, is revealed in Jesus Christ His Son, and the revelation is completed and made intelligible by the manifestation of the Holy Spirit. S. Paul expressed the practical content of GOD'S self-disclosure in his phrase "the grace of our Lord Jesus Christ, and the love of GOD, and the fellowship of the Holy Ghost." Later Christian thinkers worked it out into the doctrine of the Holy Trinity, the conception of GOD as at once Three in One, and One in Three.

To the plain man the doctrine of the Holy Trinity is something of a puzzle—on the face of it an arithmetical paradox; suggestive, moreover, of the abstract subtleties of speculation rather than of the concrete realities of religious life. But the doctrine did not have its origin, as a matter of historical fact, in any perverse love of subtlety or speculation. It certainly arose out of living realities of spiritual experience. It arose as the result of an attempt, on the part of the earliest Christian believers, to think out the meaning of what had happened in their religious lives, and to express it in speech and thought. What was this thing that had come to them, this thing which had changed their whole outlook upon the world, which had transformed their very inmost souls and made them new men, full of a new vision and a new hope? Something tremendous had happened in their lives. They were confident that it held the secret of all life, for them and for others. It was a new, an overwhelming, a conclusive revelation of GOD. They proclaimed it: they were constrained also to think about it. They had to find ways of expressing it. They had to think out what it meant.

There was Jesus Christ. Who was He? What did He mean? What was His relation to man, and to GOD? Certainly He had shed light upon GOD, and upon GOD'S nature. Through His teaching, His character, His life and death, the conception of GOD was filled with a new meaning. In Him GOD was revealed with a fulness that had never been before. He disclosed more of GOD'S inmost character, and more of the relation which He bears to men. "He that hath seen Me hath seen the Father"—the disciples felt that this witness was true. By admitting to their thought of GOD all that the life of Jesus brought, they filled with fresh glory Christ's favourite word for GOD—"your Father which is in Heaven."

In Jesus, they felt, GOD was expressed: His relationship to GOD was unique. They found the Divine in Him as in no other. They knew that GOD was in that life because He had spoken and acted there. "Through the eyes of Jesus" GOD looked out upon the world, and in Jesus' love and purity and yearning for the sinful and the heavy-laden, GOD Himself became visible. They knew now what GOD was like. GOD was like Christ. It was His glory that shone in Jesus' face. It was a new vision of Him when "Jesus of Nazareth passed by." In the grace—that is, the beauty, the glory and attractiveness—of the Lord Jesus Christ they saw a revelation of the love of GOD, a love that yearned over the fallen and the sorrowful, a love that suffered, and through suffering brought redemption.

But there was something more. It was not simply that in Jesus Christ GOD had been brought near, so that they felt they knew GOD as never before. There was in the experience which had come to them more than simply a Revealer and a Revealed. There was the Spirit which took possession of them, a transforming inward Power: a Power able to reproduce in them, by a process of growth from more to more, that character of Christ in whose lineaments they had discerned the nature of the eternal GOD Himself. There was a Presence abiding in their midst, dwelling within them, a Breath of the Divine Life which every Christian knew: a Presence which brought strength and comfort, power and love and discipline, and bore fruits of love and joy and peace. Who or what was it? An influence from on high? Yes: but it seemed more intimate, more personal than any mere "influence," more indissolubly one with them, knitting them into a fellowship in which they were united with the Father and the Son. "Truly our fellowship is with the Father, and with His Son Jesus Christ." The Spirit which bore such fruits in them, which brought them into so intimate a fellowship with GOD in Christ, they recognized as the Spirit of GOD, as the Presence in them of very GOD Himself. GOD, they felt, was not a Being far off, an Influence telling upon men from a distance. He was the very secret of life, "closer than breathing, nearer than hands and feet," so that each soul was meant to be a sacred "temple of GOD," "GOD abiding in him and he in GOD." GOD came in the Son, GOD had come also and equally in the Spirit. The Eternal Source of all things, who was known and worshipped as the Living One even before Christ came, was made more fully known in Christ, and now He was still more intimately made known in the inmost spiritual life of every day.

That was Christian experience. That was the experience out of which the doctrine of the Trinity arose. It arose out of an attempt to think the thing out. If we to-day find the doctrine difficult, at least the experience was and is both simple and profound. And we cannot help thinking about it.

It may be that sometimes we think we would rather be content to say simply with S. John that "GOD is Love." And that is truly the simplest of Christian creeds. If we were able fully to understand it, it would be sufficient. "Holy Trinity, whatever else it may signify, is a mode of saying 'Holy Love.'" But as a matter of fact it is only through the revelation of the grace of the Lord Jesus Christ and the fellowship of the Holy Spirit that we can ever come to understand the love of GOD. In the Christian Gospel GOD is revealed first as Father, secondly as Sufferer, thirdly as the Spirit of eternally victorious Life: and it takes the whole threefold revelation to express with any fulness the rich wonder of what is meant by saying that GOD is Love. Our minds cannot help passing from the contemplation of the threefold character of GOD'S self-revelation to the thought of a certain threefoldness in GOD Himself. We have to find room and place for such a thought–the thought that GOD is eternally Love, that He is eternally Father, Son, and Spirit–and yet at the same time not depart from the fundamental Christian conviction that GOD is One.

It is to be feared that many Christian people do sometimes come dangerously near to believing in three separate Gods, and what we call Unitarianism is a one-sided protest against such a tendency. GOD is indeed a unity: and so far Unitarianism is right. But Unitarianism is less than the full Christian faith in GOD, because it fails to do justice to the full riches of Christian experience, the many-sided wonder of GOD revealed in Christ, and made real to us here and now by the operation of the Spirit in our hearts. We are driven to say that GOD is not only One, but Three in One.

Nevertheless, if any one finds the theory of the Holy Trinity difficult let him not be overmuch dismayed. Let him learn to know GOD as Father and Jesus Christ as Lord and Saviour: let him learn to know the Holy Spirit as an energy of eternal life and inspiration in his heart. He will then be in effect a Trinitarian believer, even though the theologians seem to him to talk a language which he does not understand: even though—to tell the truth—he is not greatly interested by what they say.

At the same time, there is need that people should think out the meaning of the Christian revelation of GOD: perhaps that they should think it out afresh. It is possible to be technically orthodox and correct in doctrine and yet to miss the true reality of what GOD means. The conception of GOD as Father implies that GOD has eternally a Son: the life of Jesus Christ as Son of God reveals to us the quality of that Divine Fatherhood to which His Sonship corresponds. The Spirit, as the Divine Energy proceeding from the Father and the Son, is the assurance that the life of GOD can never be self-contained or aloof, but is for ever going forth from Himself, so as to be eternally operative and active, alike in the processes of Nature and in the lives of men. For "the Spirit of the Lord filleth the world," and the Divine Wisdom "reacheth from one end to the other mightily, and sweetly ordereth all things."

It follows that Christianity, the religion of the Spirit, can never stand still. Not stagnation, but life, is its characteristic note, even "that Eternal Life which was with the Father, and hath been manifested unto us." The Church which is truly alive unto GOD, and aflame with the spirit of allegiance to Him who for the joy that was set before Him endured the Cross, the Church which is truly quickened and inspired by the Spirit of Truth and Love and Power, will always be ready to "live dangerously" in the world, not shrinking timorously from needed change or experiment, not holding aloof from conflict and adventure and movement, but facing courageously all new situations and new phases whether of life or of thought as they arise, shirking no issues, welcoming all new-found truth, bringing things both new and old out of her treasure-house, so that she may both "prove all things" and also "hold fast that which is good."

There are conceptions of GOD proclaimed from Christian pulpits which are less than the full Christian conception of GOD. The GOD who is eternal Energy and Life and Love, the GOD who is revealed in Christ, and whose Spirit is the Spirit of

Freedom and Brotherhood and Truth, is neither the tyrant God of the Calvinist, nor the dead-alive God of the traditionalist, nor the obscurantist God of those who would decry knowledge and quench the Spirit. Neither, again, is GOD the God of militarists, a God who delights in carnage—even though it should be the carnage of Germans; or the God who is thought of by His worshippers as being mainly the God of the sacristy, a kind of "supreme Guardian of the clerical interest in Europe." Least of all is GOD the commonplace deity of commonplace people, a sort of placid personification of respectability, the GOD whose religion is the religion of "the Conservative Party at prayer."

He is a consuming Energy of Life and Fire. His eyes are "eyes of Flame," and His inmost essence a white-hot passion of sacrifice and of self-giving. At the heart of His self-revelation there is a Cross, the eternal symbol of the almightiness of Love: the Cross which is the source and the secret of all true victory, and newness of life, and peace.

This, and none other, is the GOD whom truly to know is everlasting life, and whom to serve is liberty. For He it is who has made us unto Himself, with hearts that are restless until they rest in Him. To do His will is to realize the object of our existence as human beings: for it is to fulfil the purpose for which we have our being, the end for which we were created; even to glorify GOD, and to enjoy Him for ever.

Chapter V

The Problem of Evil

But are not the evil and misery of the world, is not all that which we know as "sin" and pain, in manifest contradiction to this Christian conception of a GOD of Love? Most certainly they are: and it has been the strength of Christianity from the beginning that—unlike many rival systems and philosophies, including the "Christian Science" movement of modern times—it has always faced facts, and in particular has never regarded pain and sin, disease and sorrow and death, as anything but the stubborn realities which in point of fact they are. If we ask, indeed, how and why it was that evil, whether physical or moral, originally came into the world, the Gospel returns no answer, or an answer which, at best, merely echoes the ancient mythology of Jewish traditional belief—"By the envy of the Devil sin entered into the world, and death by sin": an answer which indeed denies emphatically that evil had its origin in GOD, and declares its essential root to lie in opposition to His will, but without attempting any explanation of the difficulty of conceiving how opposition to the will of GOD is possible.

The Gospel is concerned with issues that are practical rather than strictly theoretical: and the really practical problem with regard to evil is not how it is to be explained but how it is to be overcome. If we ask how evil first arose, the only honest answer is that we do not know: though we can see how the possibility, at least, of moral evil (as distinct from mere physical pain) is implicit of necessity in the existence of moral freedom. The question is sometimes asked, "If GOD is omnipotent, why does He permit evil?" But the doctrine of Divine omnipotence is misconceived when it is interpreted to mean that GOD is able to accomplish things inherently self-contradictory. GOD is omnipotent only in the sense that He is supreme over all things, and able to do all possible things. He is not able to do impossible things: and to make man free, and yet to prevent him from doing evil if he so chooses, is a thing impossible even to GOD. Man is left free to crucify his Maker, and he has availed himself of his freedom by crucifying both his Maker and his fellow-man.

If we ask, "Why does not GOD prevent war? Why does He permit murder and cruelty and rapine?" the answer is that He could only prevent these things by dint of over-riding the will of man by force: and moreover that it is not the method of GOD to do for man what man is perfectly well able to do for himself. For wars would cease if men universally desired not to fight.

We are really raising a much more difficult question if we ask, "Why does GOD allow cancer?" And to this, it may be, there is no completely satisfactory answer to be given: though it is possible to see that cancer and other diseases have a biological function, and also to recognize that the endurance of pain in some cases (though not in all) ennobles and deepens character. The writer of the Epistle to the Hebrews does not hesitate to say of Christ Himself that He "learned obedience by the things which He suffered."

In general it must be said that Christianity does not afford any complete theoretical solution of the problem of evil: what it does is to provide a point of view which sets evil in a new light, and which is adequate for the purposes of practical life. It teaches us that physical suffering, so far as it is inevitable, is to be endured and turned to spiritual profit, as a thing which is capable of bearing fruit in the deepening and discipline of character: and that moral evil is to be overcome, by the power of the grace of GOD in Christ.

If we ask, "Why should the innocent suffer?" the Christian answer is contained in the Cross. "Christ also suffered, being guiltless": and although, if Christ were regarded simply as a man and nothing more, this fact would merely intensify the problem, the matter assumes a different complexion if Christ be regarded as the revelation of GOD. For if so, then suffering enters into the experience of GOD Himself, and so far from GOD being indifferent to the sorrow and misery of the world, He shares it, and is victorious through it. "In all their affliction, He was afflicted." GOD is Himself a Sufferer, the supreme Sufferer of all, and finds through suffering the instrument of His triumph. But if this be true, then all suffering everywhere is set in a new and a transfiguring light, for it assumes the character of a challenge to become partaker in the sufferings and triumph of the Christ. "Can ye drink of the Cup that I drink of?"

So interpreted, suffering ceases to be a ground of petulance or of complaint. It is discovered to have a value. It is judged to be worth while. And it is possible to find in such a faith the grounds of a conviction that behind and beneath all suffering is the love which redeems it and the purpose which shall one day justify it, and that in very truth no sparrow falls to the ground without the Heavenly Father's knowledge and care.

Chapter VI

Sin and Redemption

The Gospel affirms that men are called to be sons of GOD; to be perfect, as the heavenly Father is perfect. The correlative of this ideal view of man as he is meant to be is a sombre view of man as he actually is. "If we say that we have no sin we deceive ourselves, and the truth is not in us." "All have sinned, and come short of the glory of GOD."

Sin is essentially a falling short, a missing of the mark, a failure to correspond with the purpose and the will of GOD. It need not necessarily involve–though of course it does in many instances involve–the deliberate transgression of a moral law which the conscience of the individual sinner recognizes as such. There are sins of omission as well as of commission, sins of ignorance as well as of deliberate intent. The fact that the conscience of a given individual does not accuse him, that he is not aware of himself as a sinner before GOD, is no evidence of his moral perfection, but rather the reverse. Jesus Christ, who possessed the surest as well as the sanest moral judgment the world has ever known, held deliberately that the open and acknowledged sinner, just because he was aware of his condition, was in a more hopeful spiritual state than the man who through ignorance of his own shortcomings believed himself to be righteous. The Pharisee, who compared himself with others to his own advantage, was condemned in the sight of GOD. The Publican, who would not so much as lift up his eyes unto heaven, but judging himself and his deeds by the standard of GOD'S holiness acknowledged himself a sinner, went away justified rather than the other. It is probably true that the ordinary man to-day is not worrying about his sins: but if so, the fact proves nothing except the secularity of his ideals and the shallowness of his sense of spiritual issues. It means, in short, that he has not taken seriously the standard of Christ. For the measure of a man's sin is simply the measure of the contrast between his character and the character of Christ.

It is likely enough that many of us will never discover that we are sinners until we have deliberately tried and failed to follow Christ. The moment we do try seriously to follow Him, we become conscious of the presence within ourselves of "that horrid impediment which the Churches call sin." We discover that we are spiritually impotent: that there is that in us which is both selfish and self-complacent: that there is a "law of sin in our members" which is in conflict with the "law of the Spirit of life": and that "we have no power of ourselves to help ourselves." We are at the mercy of our own character, which has been wrongly moulded and formed amiss by the sins and follies, the self-indulgences and the moral slackness of our own past behaviour. We are, indeed, "tied and bound by the chain of our sins."

To have realized so much is to have reached the necessary starting- point of any fruitful consideration of the Christian Gospel of redemption. The appeal of the Cross of Christ is to the human consciousness of sin; and the first effect of a true appreciation of the meaning of the Cross is to deepen in us the realization of what sin really is. The crucifixion of Christ was not the result of any peculiarly unexampled wickedness on the part of individuals. It was simply the natural and inevitable result of the moral collision between His ideals and those of society at large. The chief actors in the drama were men of like passions with ourselves, who were actuated by very ordinary human motives. It is indeed easy for men to say, "If we had been in the days of our fathers, we would not have been partakers with them in the blood of the prophets": but in so saying they are merely being witnesses unto themselves that they are the children of them which killed the prophets. Are we indeed so far removed beyond the reach of the moral weakness which yields against its own better judgment to the clamorous demands of public opinion, as to be in a position to cast stones at Pilate? Are we so exempt from the temptation to turn a dishonest penny, or to throw over a friend who has disappointed us, as to recognize no echo of ourselves in

Judas? Have we never with the Sanhedrin allowed vested interests to warp our judgment, or resented a too searching criticism of our own character and proceedings, or sophisticated our consciences into a belief that we were offering GOD service when as a matter of fact we were merely giving expression to the religious and social prejudices of our class? Have we never, like the crowds who joined in the hue- and-cry, followed a multitude to do evil? There appears in the midst of a society of ordinary, average men–men such as ourselves–a Man ideally good: and He is put to death as a blasphemer. That is the awful tragedy of the Crucifixion. What does it mean? It means that a new and lurid light is thrown upon the ordinary impulses of our mind. It means that we see sin to be exceeding sinful. That is the first salutary fruit of a resolute contemplation of the Cross.

The Cross shows us, in a word, what we are doing when we sin: consciously or unconsciously, we are crucifying that which is good. If we are able to go further, and by faith to discover in the character and bearing of the Son, crucified upon the Cross, the revelation of the heart of the Eternal Father, there dawns upon our minds a still more startling truth: consciously or unconsciously, we are crucifying GOD. Assuming, that is to say, that GOD is such as Christianity declares Him to be, holy, righteous, ideal and perfect Love, caring intensely for every one of His creatures and having a plan and a purpose for each one, then every failure of ours to correspond with the purpose of His love, every falling short of His ideal for us, every acknowledged slackness and moral failure in our lives, much more every wilful and deliberate transgression of the moral law, is simply the addition of yet a further stab to the wounds wherewith Love is wounded in the house of His friends. "Father, forgive them; they know not what they do"–the words of the Crucified are the revelation of what is in fact the eternal attitude of GOD: they are the expression of a love that is wounded, cut to the heart and crucified, by the lovelessness, the ingratitude, the tragedy of human sin, but which nevertheless, in spite of the pain, is willing to forgive.

But the Cross is no mere passivity. It is more than simply a revelation of Divine suffering, of the eternal patience of the love of GOD. It is the expression of GOD in action: a deed of Divine self- sacrifice: a voluntary taking upon Himself by man's Eternal Lover of the burden of man's misery and sin. There is a profound truth in the saying of S. Paul, that the Son of GOD "loved me, and gave Himself for me": as also in S. Peter's words about the Christ "who His own self bare our sins in His own body on the Tree, that we, being dead to sins, should live unto righteousness." There is no need to import into the phrases of the New Testament writers the crude transactional notions of later theology, no need to drag in ideas about penalties and punishments. The sole and sufficient penalty of sin is simply the state of being a sinner [2] : and the conception of vicarious "punishment" is not merely immoral, but unintelligible. Vicarious suffering, indeed, there is: an enormous proportion of the sufferings of mankind—and the sufferings of Christ are a conspicuous case in point—arise directly as the result of others' sin and may be willingly borne for others' sake. And Christ died because of His love for men, and as the expression of the love of GOD for men. He who "wholly like to us was made "sounded the ultimate depths of the bitterest experience to which sin can lead, even the experience of being forsaken of GOD." So GOD loved the world."

Regarded thus, the Cross is at once a potent instrument for bringing men to repentance, and also the proclamation of the free and royal forgiveness of men's sins by the heavenly Father. "What the law could not do, in that it was weak through the flesh, GOD sending His own Son, in the likeness of sinful flesh, and for sin, condemned sin in the flesh: that the righteousness of the law might be fulfilled in us, who walk not after the flesh, but after the Spirit."

---

[2] Sin, of course, may involve consequences, and the consequences may be both irrevocable and bitter; nor is it denied that fear of consequences may operate as a deterrent from certain kinds of sin. What is denied is that such consequences are rightly to be described as "punishment."

Forgiveness must be received on the basis of repentance and confession as the free and unmerited gift of GOD in Christ: but the redemption which Christ came to bring to men does not stop short at the bare gift of initial forgiveness. The Cross cannot rightly be separated from the Resurrection, nor the Resurrection from the bestowal of the Spirit. The forgiveness of past transgressions carries with it also the gift of a new life in Christ and the power of the indwelling Spirit to transform and purify the heart. And this is a life-long process—a process, indeed, which extends beyond the limits of this present life. The old Adam dies hard, and the victory of the spirit over the flesh is not lightly won. In the life-story of every Christian there are repeated falls: there is need of a fresh gift of forgiveness ever renewed. It is only over stepping-stones of their dead selves that men are enabled to rise to higher things. But already in principle the victory is won. "In all these things we are more than conquerors through Him that loved us." We see in Christ the first-fruits of redeemed humanity, the one perfect response on the side of man to the love of GOD. And through Christ, our Representative, self-offered to the Father on our behalf, we are bold to have access with confidence unto the throne of GOD and in Him to offer ourselves, that so we may obtain mercy, and find grace to help in time of need.

Chapter VII

The Church and Her Mission in the World

The GOD and Father of Jesus Christ loves every human being individually, cares for each and has a specific vocation for each one to fulfil. This doctrine of the equal preciousness in the sight of GOD of all human souls is for Christianity fundamental. But the correlative of Divine fatherhood is human brotherhood: just because GOD is love, and fellowship is life and heaven, and the lack of it is hell, GOD does not redeem men individually, but as members of a brotherhood, a Church.

The Church is simply the people of GOD. It is the fellowship of redeemed mankind, the community of all faithful people throughout this present world and in the sphere of the world beyond—one, holy, apostolic (i.e. missionary), and catholic, that is, universal. Death is no interruption in that Society, race is no barrier, and rank conveys no privilege. "There is neither Greek nor Jew, circumcision nor uncircumcision, Barbarian, Scythian, bond nor free: but Christ is all, and in all": over the Church the gates of Death prevail not: and "ye are all one Man in Christ Jesus."

Furthermore, the Church is described as the Body, that is, the embodiment, of Christ: the instrument or organ whereby the Spirit of Christ works in the world. Her several members are individually limbs or members in that Body, and their individual gifts and capacities, whatever they may be, are to be dedicated and directed to the service of the Body as a whole, and not to any sectional or selfish ends or purposes. In practical churchmanship, rightly understood, is to be discovered the clue to the meaning and purpose of human life.

Again, the Church is by definition international. The several races and nationalities of mankind have each their specific and individual contribution to make to the Church's common life, in accordance with their specific national temperaments and genius. All of them together are needed to give adequate expression in

36

human life to the many-sided riches of GOD in Christ. The Church is incomplete so long as a single one remains outside. The idea, therefore, of a so-called "National" Church, as a thing isolated and self-contained, is intrinsically absurd.

Therefore also the Church is missionary. She exists in order to proclaim to all the world the Good News of the love of GOD. She exists to bring all men everywhere under the scope of Christ's redemption, and to claim for the Spirit of Christ the effectual lordship over all human thought and life and activity. It is her threefold task at once to develop and make real within her own borders the life of brotherhood in Christ, to evangelize the heathen by declaring to them the satisfaction of their instinctive search for GOD in the answering search of GOD for them, and to labour for the discovery and application of Christian solutions to the problems of industry and commerce, of politics and social life and international affairs.

In so far as the Church has been true to the Spirit of Christ she has succeeded; in so far as she has made compromises with the world, and in every generation has in greater or less degree been disloyal to the standards of her Master, she has failed. In every generation there has been partial and obvious failure, side by side with real, if partial and in some ways less immediately obvious, success. But the Church can never wholly fail and must one day wholly succeed, for the reason that behind her is the omnipotence of the love of GOD.

Chapter VIII

Protestant and Catholic

The last chapter sketched the ideal of the Church and her essential mission. The realization of that ideal in the existing Church, visibly embodied here in earth is extremely fragmentary and imperfect. The Church that is one, and holy, and apostolic, and catholic, the brotherhood in Christ of all mankind, knit into unity by the fellowship of the Holy Spirit, remains a vision of the future, though a vision which, once seen, mankind will never relinquish until it be accomplished. "I believe in the Holy Catholic Church," it has been said, "but I regret that she does not as yet exist."

What does exist is a bewildering multiplicity of competing "denominations," whose points of difference are to the plain man obscure, but whose mutual separation is in his eyes an obvious scandal and an offence both against charity and against common sense. Why cannot they agree to sink their differences, and to unite upon the broad basis of a common loyalty to Christ? To what purpose is this overlapping and conflict? The reluctant tribute of the ancient sceptic—"See how these Christians love one another"—has become the modern worldling's cynical and familiar jibe; and when to the spectacle of Christian disunion is added the observation that professing Christians of all denominations appear to differ from other men, for the most part, "solely in their opinions" and not in their lives, the impulse to cry "A plague upon all your Churches" may seem all but irresistible.

Yet the problem is not susceptible of any cheap or hasty solution. Unity is the Church's goal; but the Church cannot arrive at unity by mere elimination of differences. Agreement to differ is not unity: an agreement to pretend that the differences were not there would not even be honest. What is needed is a sympathetic study of the divergent traditions and principles which lie behind existing differences, with a view to discovering which are really differences of principle, and which rest merely upon prejudice.

Unity, when it comes, can only be based upon mutual understanding and synthesis. The task will not be easy, and the time is not yet.

Meanwhile the individual's first duty is to be loyal in the first instance[3] to the spiritual tradition and discipline of the "denomination" to which he in fact belongs, unless and until he is led to conclude that some other embodies a fuller and more synthetic presentation of religious truth. It is a mistake for a man to be content either to remain in ignorance of his own immediate spiritual heritage or to refuse to try to understand what is distinctive and vital in the religious heritage of others. Most fatal of all is the attempt to combine personal loyalty to Christ with the repudiation of organized Christianity as a whole. True loyalty to Christ most certainly involves common religious fellowship upon the basis of common membership in the people of GOD.

As a matter of fact, so soon as the various sects and denominations into which modern Western Christianity is divided are seriously examined, they are seen to fall into three main types or groups. Standing by herself is the Church of Rome, venerable, august, impressive in virtue of her unanimity, her coherence, her ordered discipline, and her international position, representing exclusively the ancient Catholic tradition, and making for herself exclusive claims. At the opposite end of the scale there are the multitudinous sects of Protestantism, differing mutually among themselves but tending (as some observers think) to set less and less store by their divergences and to develop towards some kind of loosely-knit federation—a more or less united Evangelical Church upon an exclusively Protestant basis. Between the two stands the Church of England, reaching out a hand in both directions, presenting to the superficial observer the appearance of a house divided against itself; representing nevertheless, according to her true ideal, a real attempt to synthesize the essentials of Catholicism with what is both true and positive in the Protestant tradition.

---

[3] Of course in the last resort no loyalty is due to any lesser authority than that of truth, wheresoever it is found and whatsoever it turns out to be.

Protestantism stands for the liberty of the individual, for freedom of thought and of inquiry, for emphasis upon the importance of vital personal religion, for the warning that "forms and ceremonies" are of no value in themselves, but only in so far as they are the expression and vehicle of the spirit. Protestantism proclaims the liberty of Christian prophesying, the free and unimpeded access of every human soul to the heavenly Father, the spiritual equality of all men in the sight of GOD. The Protestant tradition is jealous for the evangelical simplicity of the Gospel, and in general may be said to represent the principle of democracy in religion.

Catholicism, on the other hand, bears witness to the glory of Churchmanship, to the importance of corporate loyalty to the Christian Society, to the value of sacramentalism, and the rich heritage of ancient devotional traditions, of liturgical worship and ordered ecclesiastical life. For Catholicism rites and sacraments are not anomalies, strange "material" excrescences upon a religion otherwise "spiritual." They are themselves channels and media of the Spirit's operation, vehicles of life and power.

Catholicism is more inclusive than Protestantism, including, indeed, some things which Protestants are apt to insist should be excluded. The future would seem to lie neither with the negations of pure Protestantism nor with a Catholicism wholly unreformed; but rather with a liberalized Catholicism which shall do justice to the truth of the Protestant witness. For the present the best opportunity for the working out of such a liberalized Catholicism is to be found within the Church of England: and it is from the point of view of an English Churchman that the remainder of this book will be written.

Chapter IX

Sacraments

It is sometimes asked whether the sacraments of the Christian Church are two or more than two in number. The answer depends in part upon how the term "sacrament" is defined. But the wisest teaching is that which recognizes in particular sacraments–such as Baptism and the Supper of the Lord–the operation of a general principle which runs throughout all human experience, in things both sacred and profane. "I have no soul," remarked a well-known preacher on a famous occasion, "I have no soul, because I am a soul: I have a body." It would be difficult to express more aptly the principle of sacraments, or–what comes to the same thing–the true relationship of the material to the spiritual order.

We are accustomed, in the world as we know it, to distinguish "spirit" from "matter": and we are tempted, by the mere fact that we draw a distinction between them, to think and speak at times as though spirit and matter were necessarily opposed. This is a great mistake. Matter, so far from being the opposite or the contradiction of spirit, is the medium of its expression, the vehicle of its manifestation. Spirit and matter are correlatives, but the ultimate reality of the world is spiritual. It is the whole purpose and function of matter to express, to embody, to incarnate, the Spirit. The preacher, therefore, was quite right. "I am a soul": that is, I am a personality, a spirit: and to say that is to give expression to the fundamental truth of my existence: I am a soul, and I am not a body. But "I have a body": that is, my personality is embodied or incarnate: I have a body which serves as the vehicle or instrument of my life as a man here upon earth: a body which is the organ of my spirit's self-expression and the medium both of my life's experience and of my intercourse with other men. I think, and my thoughts are mediated by movements of the brain. I speak, and the movements of my vocal chords set up vibrations and sound-waves which, impinging upon the nerves of another's ear, affect in turn another's brain: and the process, regarded from the point of view of the physiologist or the scientific observer, is a physical process through and through: yet it mediates from my mindto the mind of him who hears me a meaning which is wholly spiritual.

This principle of the mediation of the spiritual by the material is the principle of sacramentalism. It is the principle of incarnation, which runs throughout the world. The body is in this sense the sacrament of the spirit, sound is the sacrament of speech, and language the sacrament of thought. So in like manner water is the sacrament of cleansing, hands laid upon a man's head are the sacrament of authority or of benediction, food and drink are the sacrament of life. All life and all experience are in a true sense sacramental, the inward ever seeking to reveal itself in and through the outward, the outward deriving its whole significance from the fact that it expresses and mediates the spirit: so it is that a gesture—a bow or a salute—may be a sacrament of politeness, a handshake the sacrament of greeting and of friendship, the beauty of nature a sacrament of the celestial beauty, the world a sacrament of GOD.

It is in the light of this general principle of sacraments that the specific sacraments of Christianity are to be understood. In Baptism the water of an outward washing is the sacrament both of initiation into a spiritual society, and also of the cleansing and regenerating power of GOD. In Confirmation the Church's outward benediction, of which the Bishop is the minister, is the sacrament of an inward gift of spiritual strength. In Absolution words outwardly pronounced by human lips are a sacrament of Divine forgiveness and a pledge to assure us thereof. In the Eucharist the outward elements of food and drink are the sacramental embodiment of Christ and the vehicles of His outpoured life. Other sacraments, or rites commonly reckoned sacramental, we need not here particularly consider. [4]

---

[4] Matrimony and Holy Orders are discussed in different connexions elsewhere in this book. The sacrament of Unction, by which is meant the Anointing of the Sick with oil in the name of the Lord with a view to their recovery (to be

Baptism and Confirmation Baptism is the sacrament of Christian initiation, whereby a man is made visibly a member of the Christian fellowship. Converts were originally baptized in adult life, as they are to-day in the mission field. The candidate publicly renounced his heathen past and made a profession of his faith in Christ and his desire to be loyal to His Church. As a sinner in need of redemption he went down into the water, and was three times immersed in the Name of the Father, and of the Son, and of the Holy Ghost. The rite conveyed an assurance of the forgiveness of sins. The going down into the water symbolized the burial of the dead past. The coming up out of the water expressed the idea of resurrection to newness of life in Christ. The new-made Christian was said to be born again of water and of the Spirit: the "old Adam" was slain, the "new man" raised up. The candidate was henceforward a "member of Christ," a "child of GOD," an "inheritor of the Kingdom of Heaven." He was admitted both to the privileges and to the responsibilities of Church membership. It remained only that he should walk worthily of his Christian profession, and to this end hands were laid upon his head in benediction, with prayer that he might be made strong by the indwelling power of the Holy Spirit. Confirmation was thus the complement of Baptism, and the two things normally went together. The same order is still commonly observed to- day in the case of persons baptized in adult life, and has the advantage of making the significance of both rites, and their mutual relation, at once more vivid and more intelligible.

But the question arose, in the second Christian generation, of the status of children in relation to the Church. Might children be admitted to membership in infancy, or must they wait until they were adult? The Church decided that they were admissible, provided there were reasonable assurance that they would be Christianly brought up. Why should a child grow up in

---

distinguished from the mediaeval and modern Roman use of "Extreme Unction" as a preparation for death), has been revived sporadically within the Church of England in recent times, but is not usually for the plain man of more than academic importance or interest.

heathenism? Had not the Lord said, "Suffer the little children to come unto Me, and forbid them not"? There seemed no reason why children should not be brought at once within the sphere of Christian regeneration.

But if children were baptized in infancy, it was plainly essential that they should at a later stage receive systematic instruction in Christian faith and practice; and the Western Church (though not the Eastern) adopted the practice of separating Confirmation from Baptism, and deferring the former until such instruction had been received. The plan has obvious advantages, though it tends to obscure in some respects the essential meaning of Confirmation and its original close relation to the sacrament of Baptism.

In modern usage Baptism is normally administered by a priest, Confirmation always by a Bishop. Candidates are received by the latter upon the assurance of one of his subordinate clergy that they are adequately instructed and rightly disposed by faith and penitence to receive the gifts of the Holy Ghost—"the spirit of wisdom and understanding, the spirit of counsel and might, the spirit of knowledge and of the fear of the Lord." As an immediate preliminary to the actual rite the candidate solemnly and deliberately declares his acceptance of the obligations and implications of his baptism. The laying on of hands which follows is in one aspect the recognition by the Bishop, as chief pastor of the flock of Christ in his own diocese, that the candidate is henceforward of communicant status. In another aspect it is the bestowal through prayer of a fuller gift of the Holy Ghost, whereby the candidate is "confirmed" (_i.e. made strong). It should be noted that the Bishop's prayer for each candidate is not that he may be made magically perfect there and then, but that he may "daily increase" in GOD'S Holy Spirit "more and more," until he come to GOD'S "everlasting Kingdom."

The Sacrament of Repentance It must be admitted that very large numbers of those who are confirmed lapse at an early stage in their lives from the communion of the Church and never return.

The causes of this are various, and there is no one sovereign or universal remedy. Sometimes it is to be feared that there has been either lack of intelligence or lack of thoroughness in the candidates' preparation. In not a few cases what has really happened is that the young communicant has been led into the commission of some sin of a kind which his own conscience recognizes as grave, so that he feels that he has spoilt his record and failed to "live up to" his profession. To go back to communion, he thinks, would in these circumstances be a kind of mockery. Unfortunately he does not know—since too often he has not been taught—any effectual method of spiritual recovery and renewal.

What is needed in such cases is a real doctrine and practice of Christian repentance. It is the universal teaching of the Christian Church that forgiveness is freely available for all those who truly repent. A man who, laying aside self-justification, will freely acknowledge his offences and shortcomings before GOD, and that in a spirit not of self-pity, self-loathing or self-contempt, but of sorrow at having brought discredit upon the Christian name and done what in him lies to crucify the Son of GOD afresh, may freely claim and find in Christ forgiveness and inward peace.

This Gospel or message of the forgiveness of sins it is part of the mission of the Christian Church to set forth. It is her mission to set it forth not merely as a piece of good news proclaimed in general terms to the world at large, but as a healing assurance brought home in detail, as need may require, to the individual consciences of sinners. "Whosoever sins ye remit, they are remitted unto them, and whosoever sins ye retain, they are retained." The words may have been uttered by the historical Jesus of Nazareth, or they may not— they are ascribed to the risen Christ in the Fourth Gospel. In any event they represent the Church's conviction of her authority to exercise a reconciling ministry, to remit sins and to retain them.

In early times such grave offenders as by their deeds had brought scandal upon the Christian name were excluded from

Christian fellowship until reconciled by penance; and many whose sins, being secret, might otherwise have escaped detection, preferred to make open confession of them in the Christian assembly. "Confess your faults one to another," writes S. James, "and pray one for another, that ye may be healed." The ancient system of public "penance" (_i.e. penitence) was for a time at least revived in a modern form by Wesley.[5] Its application to notorious offenders is described in the English Prayer-book as a "godly discipline," the restoration of which is "much to be wished." But it is hardly practicable under the conditions of modern Church life, and it has disadvantages as well as advantages. Its working in the early days of the Church was not found to be wholly for good.

Burdened consciences nevertheless require relief: and sin is not merely a private affair between the soul and GOD; it is also an offence against the Brotherhood. A system grew up under which the need was met by the substitution, in the majority of cases, of private for public penance. Confession was made, no longer before the whole assembly, but privately before the Bishop, whose office it was, both as pastor of the flock and as representative of the Church, to declare forgiveness or "absolution," and to restore penitents to communion. At a later date presbyters or priests were also authorized, as delegates of the Bishop for this and other purposes, to receive confessions and to absolve penitents.

In this way arose in the Church what came to be known as the sacrament of Penance, or the practice of sacramental confession. It was ranked as a sacrament for the reason that the inward assurance of GOD'S pardon is in this connexion outwardly mediated by words of Absolution audibly pronounced. In medieval times there grew up a regular system of the confessional and an elaborate science of the guidance and direction of souls. Recourse to sacramental confession was made

---

[5] The "class-meeting" of strict Wesleyanism is said to have originally involved mutual confession of sins among the members of the "class."

obligatory for all Christians at least once in the year.[6] The system came to be attended by many superstitions and abuses, frequently it was exploited in the interests of a corrupt sacerdotalism, sometimes it was associated with a degrading casuistry.

But the confessional met and meets a real human need; and while Protestantism, as a whole, broke away at the time of the Reformation in a violent reaction from the whole theory and practice of sacramental confession, the Church of England quite deliberately retained it. It was abolished as a compulsory obligation. It was made less prominent in the Church's system. But as a means of spiritual reconciliation and spiritual guidance, freely open to such as for any reason desire to make use of it, it was retained; and in the case of persons who for reasons of conscience hesitate to present themselves for Holy Communion it is specifically urged in the Book of Common Prayer as the needed remedy.[7] The words of S. John xx. 23 are quoted in the Anglican formula of ordination to the priesthood; and a form of words to be used by the priest in the private absolution of penitents is prescribed in the Office for the Visitation of the Sick.

As regards the theory of the confessional it is important to bear certain things in mind. The confession is made primarily to GOD, secondarily to His Church. The priest is the Church's accredited delegate and representative. He acts not in virtue of any magical powers inherent in himself, either as an individual or as a member of any so-called sacerdotal caste. If he declares the penitent absolved it is as pastor of the flock, and as one officially authorized by the Church to be her mouthpiece for these purposes. The ultimate absolving authority, under GOD, is the Christian Society as a whole. It is a confessor's duty to assure himself of the reality of the penitent's contrition, and to enjoin that restitution or amends shall be made for any wrong which has been done, in all cases in which amends or restitution is possible.

---

[6] This is still the formal rule of the Church of Rome.

[7] See the closing paragraph of the first of the three lengthy exhortations to Holy Communion, printed immediately after the "Prayer for the Church Militant" in the Prayer- book.

He may also give advice and counsel for the guidance of the spiritual life; and it is customary to enjoin the performance of a "penance," which in modern practice usually takes the form of some minor spiritual exercise of a more or less remedial kind. The acceptance of the penance is regarded as an enacted symbol of submission to the Church's judgment. (The mediaeval theory that the penance is of the nature of a punishment or penalty imposed by the Church upon her erring members ought, I think, to be repudiated. It is perhaps permissible to differ from the moral theology of Borne in holding that it is not essential to impose a penance at all, while recognizing the value in most cases of suggesting some definite act of self-discipline or observance, of a kind adapted to the penitent's circumstances and needs). The confessor is, of course, bound in the strictest way not to reveal anything said to him in confession, or to broach the subject again to the penitent without the latter's express permission, or to allow his subsequent manner or behaviour to be influenced in any the least degree by what has been confessed.

It is highly unfortunate that the practice of sacramental confession should have been made the subject of controversy, and as a consequence of this that the Church's teaching with regard to it should have been either unhealthily suppressed or obtruded out of season. There are without doubt numerous cases in which such a spiritual remedy is badly needed. There are burdened souls needing absolution and there are perplexed souls needing guidance. What is desirable is that the actual teaching of the Church of England on this subject should be plainly and frankly set before her members, and that opportunities should be afforded them of making their confessions if they desire or need to do so. It is the plain duty of a parish priest to provide such opportunities for his people. He is as plainly going beyond his duty if he tries to enforce the practice of sacramental confession as a necessary obligation. There are differences of opinion as to how widespread is the spiritual need to which confession ministers. There are reasons for thinking that it is more widespread than is commonly recognized. But it is of vital importance that no one should be pressed or brow-beaten into going to confession, or should do so, in any circumstances, otherwise than by his own voluntary act.

The Sacrament of Holy Communion Throughout Christian history and in all parts of Christendom the central and highest focus of Christian worship and devotion, and the great normal vivifying channel of spiritual renewal and power, has been the sacrament of Holy Communion. It has been celebrated amid great diversities of liturgy and ritual and circumstance, and has been known by many different names and titles—mass, eucharist, communion, sacrifice: essentially it is one thing—the sacrament of the Body and Blood of Christ.

The Gospels record that at the Last Supper on the night of His betrayal the Lord Jesus took bread and blessed and broke it, saying, "Take, eat: this is My Body, which is for you: do this in remembrance of Me": and that in like manner He took a Cup of mingled wine and water, and when He had given thanks He gave it to them, saying, "This Cup is the New Covenant in My Blood, which is shed for you and for many for the remission of sins: do this, as often as ye shall drink it, in remembrance of Me."

With the exceptions of the Society of Friends and the Salvation Army, every existing "denomination" of Christians has continued in one form or another the observance of this Mystical Meal. In the Roman Church, and in many parishes of the Church of England, it is celebrated daily; and it is evident from the provisions of her Prayer-book that the Church of England intends that there shall be a celebration of the Communion in all normal parishes at least on all Sundays and Holy Days.

Historically the institution of the weekly Eucharist is deeply rooted in the tradition of the Church, and is the origin of the Christian Sunday, The Christians met together week by week to keep on the day of the Lord's rising that memorial of the crucified yet risen Christ which is also Christ's gift of Himself to men. It would have seemed unthinkable in the early days of Christianity for any baptized Christian, who was not prevented by unavoidable circumstances from being present, to be absent on the Lord's Day from the Lord's Table. It ought to be equally unthinkable to-day.

With regard to the significance of the Sacrament, a man's view is necessarily coloured partly by his own experience as a communicant, and partly by the extent to which he is disposed to attach weight to the devotional traditions of Christendom as a whole; and it is worth remembering that forms of teaching about Holy Communion which are intellectually crude may represent a real, though an infelicitous, attempt to express in thought certain elements in eucharistic experience which are deep and real, and to which more attenuated types of doctrine fail to do justice.

The celebration of the Eucharist is from one point of view an enacted drama, a doing over again in the name and in the person of Christ of that which Christ did in His own person on the night of the Last Supper. Bread is taken and blessed and broken and offered to GOD in thanksgiving: Wine in like manner is poured out and blessed and offered together with the Bread. And the Bread and the Wine symbolize the Body and the Blood of Christ—the Body that was broken and the Blood that was shed—the life that was freely given for the life of the world.

The whole drama of the Eucharist is thus deeply symbolical; but the Bread and the Wine are more than mere symbols in the modern sense of that word. They are a sacrament of Christ Himself, who by means of them manifests His presence in the midst of His worshipping disciples to be the Bread of life and the Food of souls. "This is My Body"—that is, "This embodies Me: where this is, I am: receiving this, you receive Me." "This is My Blood"—that is, "This is My life: My life which is given for you: My life which in death I laid down and in rising again from the dead I resumed: My life which is to be the principle of spiritual life in you." "Except ye eat the flesh of the Son of Man, and drink His blood, ye have no life in you. Whoso eateth My flesh and drinketh My blood, hath eternal life.... He that eateth My flesh and drinketh My blood, dwelleth in Me and I in him."

There is, then, in the communion of the Body and Blood of Christ a manifestation of Christ's Real Presence, a spiritual

Presence indeed, which is discerned by the spiritual vision of Christian faith, but a Presence of which the reality is independent of individual faithlessness, though not independent of the faith of the Christian Church as a whole.

This doctrine of the Real Presence (as it is called) of course does not imply that Christ is absent from His Church at other times or in other connexions. We believe that all times and places are present to the mind of Christ, and that therefore at all times and in all places we are in His presence. We believe, further, that Christ through the Spirit is embodied, however inadequately, in His Church, and that He dwells spiritually in the hearts of Christian men. There is nothing, however, in these truths to exclude the further truth that His presence is specially manifested through the Bread which embodies Him and the Wine which is His Blood. Bread and wine, solemnly set apart for the purpose of communion and hallowed by the Spirit in response to the prayer of the Church, possess henceforward a significance which did not belong to them before. They are now vehicles or sacraments of the Body and Blood of Christ.

The purpose of the manifestation of Christ's Presence in Holy Communion is that we should receive Him, and a participation in the service which stops short of actual communion is so far incomplete. But it is gratuitous to assume that the reality of the sacramental Presence is limited to the moment of actual or individual reception, and it is untrue to say that attendance at the service, apart from individual reception, is unmeaning. The habitual attendance of persons who are not regular communicants—unless it be in the case of those who for any reason are as yet unconfirmed—falls short of full discipleship and is intrinsically undesirable. But this objection does not apply to attendance at the service on the part of communicant Churchmen who yet on a particular occasion do not communicate: and to attend throughout the service without personally communicating is a procedure infinitely preferable to the irreverent modern custom, still prevalent in too many parishes, of leaving the Church in the course of a celebration of the

Communion, and before the consecration has taken place. It is unfair to those who are preparing to receive Communion that their devotions should be disturbed by the noisy egress of a large body of worshippers. It is also quite unintelligible that any Churchman who considers seriously the meaning of the Eucharist should be content to depart before the liturgical drama has reached its climax.

As regards actual reception of Holy Communion, it is a partaking of Christ, who gives Himself therein to His disciples to be in them a spiritual principle of life and power. S. Paul discovers in the Eucharist a spiritual food and drink which is the reality to which the Manna and the Water from the Rock of Hebrew story correspond as types and shadows, and he declares that the Bread which we break is a sharing of the Body of Christ, and that the Cup of Blessing which we bless is a sharing of His Blood. At the same time the Communion is not to be interpreted in any gross or carnal manner, or in such a way as to give colour to the ancient taunt of Celsus, the heathen critic, that Christians were self-confessed cannibals. The Fourth Gospel, which, in a context that is in a general sense eucharistic, ascribes to our Lord strong phrases about the necessity of eating His flesh and drinking His blood, proceeds in the same context to explain that "it is the Spirit that giveth life," that "the flesh," in itself, "profiteth nothing." "The sayings which I have spoken unto you are spirit and are life." In other words, we are to understand that when our Lord uses the terms "flesh" and "blood" He means the Spirit of which His life in the flesh was the expression, and the Life of which His outpoured Blood was the principle: that the inward reality of the Eucharist is to be discovered, not in any quasi-material fleshly embodiment which the Bread conceals, or in any quasi-literal Blood, but rather in the Spirit and the Life of Christ Himself. The Bread is His Body in the sense that it is an embodiment of His Spirit: the Wine is His Blood in the sense that it mediates His Life. The sacrament is to be understood as a "point of personal contact with Jesus Christ." Rightly to receive Communion is to hold spiritual converse with the risen Lord and to find in Him the Bread of Life, the food and sustenance of the soul. So it is that the Eucharist, at once supremely natural and wholly supernatural, is the meeting-place of earth and heaven. From one point of view our worship is in the heavenly places in Christ Jesus. It is "with angels and archangels and with all the company of heaven," that we laud and magnify GOD'S Holy Name. We join in an eternal act of worship, which is that of the whole Church, the departed with the living, whose adoration ascends continually before the throne of GOD.

If we like to express it so, we are pleading the eternal sacrifice: we are uniting ourselves, in desire and in intention, with Christ's eternal self-devotion and oblation of Himself. Calvary itself was in a sense but the enacted symbol, the supreme outward expression, of our Lord's sacrifice, of which the inward essence is eternal. It is the self-offering of a Will that was wholly dedicated to GOD on others' behalf, obedient even unto death, and through death triumphant: the Will of One "who through the Eternal Spirit offered Himself without spot to GOD," and who now, being ascended into the heavens, for ever liveth to make intercession for us. Looking at the Eucharist from this point of view we are bold to approach the Throne of GOD and to offer Christ on our behalf–"Behold the Lamb of GOD that taketh away the sin of the world": but we proceed also to offer ourselves in Christ–"Here we offer and present unto Thee, O Lord, ourselves, our souls and bodies, to be a reasonable, holy and lively sacrifice unto Thee."

And so doing we are made one with Christ and one in Him with each other. The Eucharist has a social aspect which is too little regarded. It is the sacrament of Holy Fellowship. "We that are many are one Bread, one Body," wrote S. Paul, "for we all partake of the one Bread." The Holy Communion is the sacrament of the unity of all Christians in Christ. The scandal of a divided Christendom shows itself perhaps most of all in the fact that it prevents inter- communion. For that very reason it appears to many persons unreal, and therefore wrong, to practise isolated acts of inter-communion while ecclesiastical differences remain unresolved: it is to conceal the fact of actual disunion beneath the cloak of immediate sentiment. Yet there is a true sense in which, through the Spirit, we are, in the act of communion, made one with the fellowship of all faithful people whether in the sphere of this earthly life or in the world that is beyond death and tears: with all those, of whatever race or rank or age or country, who amid whatever diversity of language and liturgy and denominational loyalty, have named the name of Christ and received the life of Christ in obedience to His command as they understood it. There is no bond comparable to this bond, and no equality like the equality of those who, high and low, rich and poor, one with another, kneel side by side as brothers and sisters at the common Table of the Lord.

And lastly there is a further point. The Body of Christ is a broken Body and the Blood is Blood that is shed. "This is My Body which is for you"–for you, and never for Myself. The Bread is the Bread of Sacrifice and the Cup is the Stirrup-cup of Service: and part, surely, and a great part, of the meaning of the words, "Do this in remembrance of Me," is "Break your bodies in union with My Body broken: give your lives in sacrifice for others, as I have given Mine." The Eucharist, rightly regarded, is the mainspring and motive-power of service, the principle of a life that is crucified. And all those who in their day and generation have spent their lives unselfishly and used themselves up in promoting causes not their own are partakers in that Holy Fellowship.

At this present time of war and tumult, when all the powers of Hell are abroad and leagued together for the onset, we think of that which alone can be the redemption of war, even the self-devotion of those who, hating the whole devilish business and going into it only because they saw no alternative to Duty's clear and imperative call, have been counted worthy to show forth the love than which no man hath greater, even to lay down their lives for their friends. There is no one so unfortunate as not to have known some such men. And at the Communion Service "in the act of conscious incorporation into the fellowship of the love of Jesus," it may be given to us in some measure to understand these things, and to know that we are become partakers in the power of a world-wide crucifixion, a fellowship of broken bodies and lives poured out in Christ: and to know also—with a knowledge that is not of this world—that somehow, in it and through it, the Spirit of GOD in Christ will bring redemption.

So wonderful, so many-sided, and so full of meaning is this Sacrament: so great is the measure of their loss who, professing and calling themselves Christians, are content to ignore the last injunction of the Christ to His disciples on the night before He died that we might live.

Chapter X

The Last Things

"It is appointed unto men once to die, and after death the judgment."

"He shall come again in glory to judge both the quick and the dead, whose Kingdom shall have no end."

"I believe in the resurrection of the body, and the life everlasting."

Jesus Christ spoke in symbolical language of His coming in the clouds of heaven as Son of Man with power and great glory, and declared that the Divine verdict upon the lives and deeds of men should be determined by their relationship to Him and to His ideals. Both in the days of the Apostles, and for the most part among succeeding generations of Christian people down to the present time, it would seem that a more literal signification was attached to His words than they will really bear. The truth of the Divine Judgment upon men's lives nevertheless stands. "GOD is a great Judge, strong and patient: and GOD is provoked every day." We must, however, be careful, in thinking of the reality of Divine Judgment, to interpret the justice of GOD in the light of the Christian revelation of His Love. The attitude of GOD towards sinners is never anything but love, though a love that is holy and righteous, and never merely sentimental. GOD as Christ reveals Him can never impose or inflict a merely external penalty upon a sinner, other than the supreme penalty of being simply what he is, viz. a soul who by his own deliberate actions has separated himself from goodness and from GOD. It is important in thinking of the Judgment to remember that the essence of judgment is neither the sentence nor the penalty: it is simply the verdict, whereby moral and spiritual realities are revealed, shams and disguises are stripped off, and evil is separated from good. [8]If our Lord, speaking in parables, declared, of such as had neglected

---

[8] The associations of an English law-court, in which the verdict is the work of the jury, are here misleading.

to do good, that "these shall go away into eternal punishment," a considerable body of orthodox opinion in the Christian Church has always held that the punishment in question consists essentially in the "penalty of loss"—the loss of goodness and of GOD, the loss of capacity for the life which is life indeed—rather than in any imagined "penalty of sense," or purposeless prolongation of pain. The imagery which our Lord employed to describe the spiritual condition known as "hell" is taken from the Valley of Hinnom, a ravine just outside the walls of Jerusalem, in which fires were continually maintained for the destruction of refuse, and maggots preyed on offal. The imagery is sufficiently terrible; but it suggests the destruction of waste products in GOD'S creation, rather than the prolonged torture of living beings. It may well be that a soul, which by persistent and deliberate rejection of every appeal of the Divine Love even to the very end—in this life or beyond—has become so wholly self-identified with evil as to be finally incapable of life in GOD, passes, of necessity, out of sentient existence altogether. We do not know. What we do know is, in the first place, that wickedness is of its very nature instinct with the eternal quality of "hell"; and, in the second place, that GOD is Love, and that GOD "desireth not the death of a sinner, but rather that he may turn from his wickedness, and live."

Just as the term "hell" expresses the condition of a soul which by its own act and deed and deliberate choice has become wholly self- identified with evil, so the term "heaven" expresses the spiritual state of the pure in heart, to whom it is given to see GOD. So regarded, heaven is simply the ideal consummation of progressive spiritual advance, the perfect fruition of that "beatific vision" which the saints of GOD desired. It has ever been the conviction of the Christian Church that her members are already, even in this present life, made partakers in the life of heaven, just in proportion as their affections are set upon things above and not upon things in the earth. What is begun here is continued more perfectly hereafter; but it is unreasonable to assume that at the moment of death the ultimate fulness of "heaven" is immediately attained.

The Church, therefore, has believed in an intermediate state, sometimes called "Purgatory," a condition of progressive purification and spiritual growth, characterized at once by a deepening penitence for the sins and failures of the past, and by a deepening joy in GOD'S more perfect service.

Moreover, since the Christian salvation is a social salvation, those who have departed this life in GOD'S faith and fear shall not without us be made perfect. None can enter fully into the joy of the Lord until the whole of GOD'S great World-purpose is accomplished, and all are gathered in. This brings us to the consideration of the Christian belief in the Second Advent and the final Kingdom of GOD. It has already been remarked that the terms in which this belief is expressed are symbolical and should not be taken literally. Just because we ourselves, under the conditions of life here upon earth, are immersed in the stream of time, the idea of an ending of the World-process, a final passing over of time into eternity, is to us, in the strict and literal sense of the words, unthinkable. Only under the form of imagery and symbol is it in the nature of things possible for the idea of the last great Drama to be expressed, or rather, suggested: it is impossible for our minds to grasp, in any more exact or effectual manner, the Reality which the imagery is meant to symbolize. It may be that the event expressed by the dramatic picture of the Second Advent of the Christ is simply the revelation of the fact of His Eternal Presence at once as Saviour and as Judge; however this may be, the picture stands for the assurance of His final triumph, and the vindication of His Kingdom in its fulness: and as such it is the object of Christian hope—"Hallowed be Thy Name; Thy Kingdom come; Thy will be done; in earth, as it is in Heaven."

If we ask what is the positive nature of the Christian hope and what the final character of the life of heaven, the answer is that we cannot fully say, that we know only in part, "we see obscurely, as in a mirror." In hymn and ecstasy and vision men have sought to find expression for the substance of things hoped for, and they have failed. "Eye hath not seen nor ear heard, neither hath it entered into the heart of man to conceive, the things that GOD hath prepared for them that love Him." The Book of the Revelation essays to paint a picture of the heavenly state, and for the most part succeeds in setting before our minds a noble imagery; but in the end its language is most convincing when it tells us what heaven is not. "They shall hunger no more, neither thirst any more, neither shall the sun light on them, nor any heat. And GOD shall wipe away all tears from their eyes." Negatives and contrasts—the picture of a state of things contrasted with all that in the world as we know it is amiss; we cannot positively envisage heaven. Only we believe that "there remaineth a rest for the people of GOD," where nevertheless they rest not day or night from His perfect service. "Beloved, now are we sons of GOD, and it doth not yet appear what we shall be: but we know that when He shall appear we shall be like Him: for we shall see Him as He is."

Here this chapter might end: but with regard to the nature of the Christian conception of the life of the world to come there is something more to be said: for the Church's creed contains the assertion of a belief in the Resurrection of the Body, or even, in the Latin form of the Apostles' Creed, and in the translation which appears in the Prayer-book Service for Baptism, in the Resurrection of the Flesh. The plain man may be tempted, brushing aside such a doctrine in its plain and literal acceptation as a manifest impossibility, either to hold aloof from a Church which retains such an affirmation in her creed, or else to conclude hastily that the words are meant only as a picturesque way of expressing a belief in the immortality of the soul. Either attitude would be a mistake. It is true that a literal resuscitation of Christian corpses on some future Day of Resurrection would be neither possible nor desirable. Nevertheless the Christian doctrine of the life to come involves more than a bare assertion of the immortality of the soul.

The body is the embodiment or vehicle of the spirit; the spirit disembodied would be a mere wraith, a phantasm of the living man. The life of the world to come is not unreal or shadowy as compared with the concrete reality of the life of earth: it is a life richer and fuller, more concrete and more glorious than the life of earth. The Church by her doctrine of the Resurrection means to affirm that the full reality of that which made the living man what he was is carried over into the life beyond. The buried corpse is not "the body that shall be." "There is a natural body, and there is a spiritual body." As to the nature of the future embodiment of the spirit in the life beyond the grave we are ignorant. "GOD giveth it a body as it hath pleased Him, and to each seed a body of its own." But we believe that "the deeds done in the body" here upon earth while we are yet tabernacling in the flesh necessarily affect and determine the character of the spiritual embodiment which shall be ours hereafter. For this reason we hold our bodies sacred, as being temples of the Holy Ghost. "The body is not for fornication, but for the Lord; and the Lord for the body." Christianity can have nothing to do with the notion that the defilement of the body is without effect in the pollution of the soul.

[NOTE.-For a fuller treatment of the subjects of the Second Advent and the Resurrection of the Body the writer may be allowed to refer to Chapters III. and IV. in his book, Dogma, fact and Experience(Macmillan & Co., 1915).]

Chapter XI

Clergy and Laity

The clergy are not the Church. They are a specialized class within it. They are men who believe themselves to be called by GOD to give themselves for life to the particular work of caring directly for the spiritual interests of their fellows. To this end they are set apart by ordination. They hold the commission and authorization of the Church to minister the Word and Sacraments of the Gospel in the name of Christ and of the Brotherhood. Their task is high and difficult. It is not wonderful if they fail. But solemn prayer is offered for them at their ordination: and the answer to the Church's prayers is according to the measure of the Church's faith.

The historical or Catholic system of ministry in the Church consists of a hierarchy in three orders or gradations. To the order of Bishops belongs oversight or pastorate-in-chief. It is not the business of a Bishop to be prelatical, or to lord it over GOD'S heritage, but to be the servant of the servants of GOD. A Bishop is consecrated to his office by not less than three of those who are already Bishops. He exercises all the functions of the Christian ministry, including those of confirmation and ordination and the right to take part in episcopal consecrations.

Priests and deacons are a Bishop's delegates for certain purposes. A priest may have charge of a "parish" or subdivision of a diocese, and is competent to celebrate the Eucharist, to bless, to baptize, and to absolve. He is also authorized to preach, and to give instruction in Christian doctrine. He may not confirm or ordain apart from the Bishop, though he may co-operate with the latter in ordinations to the priesthood. He is ordained to his ministry by the Bishop acting in conjunction with certain representatives of the priesthood who take part with him in the laying on of hands.

Deacons are subordinate ministers appointed to assist parish priests in the work of parochial visiting and also, within certain limits, in the conduct of Divine worship and the administration of the sacraments. They may read parts of the service, but have no authority to bless or to absolve. They may preach by express and specific license from the Bishop. They may not celebrate the Eucharist, but may assist the priest who does so by reading the Gospel and administering the chalice. They are ordained to their office by the Bishop, and in most cases, though not invariably, proceed subsequently to the priesthood.[9]

The principles which underlie this system of Catholic order in the Church are important. The devolution of authority to minister through the episcopate safeguards the continuity of the Church's corporate life and tradition, and secures that ministerial functions shall be exercised in the name and by the authority of the Christian Society as a whole. Moreover through the ordered succession of the Bishops the tradition of ministerial authority is carried back certainly to sub- apostolic, and perhaps also actually to apostolic, times: it represents in principle Christ's commission to His Apostles—"As the Father hath sent Me, even so send I you."

At the same time it is important that the doctrine of the ministry should not be allowed to become "sacerdotalist" in a wrong sense. The Christian priesthood is not in possession of any magical or exclusive powers. The essence of priesthood is the dedication of life as a whole to the service of GOD on behalf of others: and in this sense every Christian man is meant in his ordinary daily life and business to be a priest of GOD and a servant of his brethren. What the Church to-day needs most chiefly is a body of laymen who will take seriously their vocation. A layman is not a Christian of inferior type, on whose behalf the clergy are expected to display a vicarious spirituality: he is simply an unordained member of the people of GOD. The hope of the future is that laymen should do their part, not merely by supporting the efforts of the clergy, but by exercising their own

---

[9] In the absence of a Bishop or priest, a deacon is competent to baptize. In the absence of any of the clergy Baptism may also, in cases of urgency, be administered by a layman, and in the absence of a man, by a woman.

proper functions as living members of Christ. The Church—and especially the Church of England—is in vital need of reform. The recently launched "Life and Liberty" Movement is a hopeful sign of the determination of a certain number of clergy and laity that reform shall be secured. In particular it is essential that the Church should recover freedom of self-government in spiritual things, and liberty to adapt her machinery and organization to changing needs, by the readjustment of her relation towards the State. This may or may not involve disestablishment, and disestablishment in turn, if it should take place, need not necessarily involve, but in practice would probably involve, some measure of partial disendowment. The Church must be prepared for all eventualities, and must be ready, should necessity arise, to take cheerfully the spoiling of her goods. For liberty is essential at all costs.

In the movement for Life and Liberty, as in every other department of her work, the Church needs the co-operation of her laity. It is their duty both to be informed in ecclesiastical affairs, and to make their voices heard. It is part of the programme of Church reformers to give the laity, through elected representatives, a more effective voice in Church affairs. The administration of finance and the raising of funds for work both at home and abroad is more particularly their province, but there is no single department of Church affairs in which the layman ought not to have his share, though no doubt the Bishops in virtue of their office have a special responsibility in matters of doctrine. Certainly there is need of a much greater extension of lay preaching, and a freer recognition of the capacity of many laymen to lead the worship and intercessions of their brethren. The administration of the sacraments, with the partial exception of baptism, is reserved for those to whom it is committed: but this need not and does not apply to the ministries of preaching and of prayer.

Clerical autocracy, where it exists, ought resolutely and firmly to be broken down. It has to be admitted that between clergy and laity at present there is a regrettable and widespread cleavage. The clergy are widely criticized, and it is certain that they have many faults. One who belongs to their number cannot help being conscious of some at least of the failings both of himself and of his class. But the faults are not all upon one side. It may be suspected that those who criticize the clergy with the greatest freedom are not always those who pray for them most earnestly. To affirm that the laity get, upon the whole, the clergy they deserve would be too hard a saying: but it is sometimes forgotten that the clergy are recruited from the ranks of the laity, and that, when not dehumanized by an undue professionalism of outlook, they are human. Many of them would be frankly grateful for friendly co-operation and criticism on the part of the lay members of their flocks. One of the difficulties about preaching is that the clergy in many instances do not really know what is in the layman's mind. The life of the Church in England will not proceed along healthy lines until there is greater mutual candour between laymen and clergy. At present laymen will not talk freely about matters of religion in the presence of the clergy because they imagine (often quite wrongly) that the latter would be shocked. It sometimes happens conversely that the clergy hesitate to express their real minds for fear that laymen would be shocked. This attitude of mutual reserve is hopeless. No Christian, lay or clerical, has any business to be shocked at any expression of opinion whatever, orthodox or unorthodox, whether in faith or in morals. Either side may disagree with the other; but either ought to be prepared to listen to what the other has to say.

Chapter XII

The Bible

The Bible is the "sacred Book" of Christianity, as the Koran is the sacred Book of Mohammedanism; with this difference, however, that Christianity, as the religion of the Spirit, can never be, like Mohammedanism, a "religion of the Book," any more than it can be, like ancient Judaism, a religion of the Law. The Biblical writings include two main collections of books, known as the Old Testament and the New Testament respectively, of which the latter alone is distinctively Christian. Intermediate between the two "Testaments" in point of date are the writings known as the "Apocrypha," which though inferior, for the most part, in spiritual value to the fully canonical books, and frequently omitted from printed editions of the Bible, are regarded by the Church as canonical in a secondary sense.

The various books of the Bible originally became canonical, that is, were included in the "canon" or collection of sacred writings, on the ground that they were read aloud or recited in the course of Divine worship. The Old Testament canon comprises the books customarily read aloud in the Jewish synagogue, together with certain other writings associated with them. The books of the New Testament are a similar collection of early Christian writings which were read side by side with the Old Testament in Christian worship. The selection of these particular writings for the purpose was determined in part by the Church's recognition of their spiritual value and in part by the regard which was paid by the Christian community to the religious authority of those by whom they were believed to have been written.

Speaking generally, we may say that the Old Testament is the religious literature of Judaism. It is the literary deposit of the spiritual life of a nation, the written record and monument of a progressive process of religious development. It begins at the level of folklore and primitive tribal cults, such as are portrayed or reflected, for example, in parts of the Pentateuch and in the Books of Judges and Samuel. It culminates, in the utterances of the greatest of the prophets and in many of the Psalms, at the highest levels of religious attainment which are discoverable anywhere in history prior to the coming of our Lord.

The Old Testament will always have a value for Christianity: in part because many of the religious lessons which it conveys can never be superseded even by Christianity itself: in part because the study of it provides the general knowledge of Judaism, and of Jewish institutions and modes of thought, which is necessary for the proper understanding of the religious background of the Gospels, and of much else in the New Testament as well: in part also because the two revelations—the Jewish and the Christian—hang together, interlocking with one another as anticipation and fulfilment, in a manner which is singularly impressive.

The various books of the Old Testament, nevertheless, require to be read by Christians with discrimination, and with a clear realization of their Jewish character. There is much in the Old Testament as it stands which is liable to mislead the simple and cause needless difficulty. There are, moreover, numerous passages, and not a few entire books, which except in the light of historical criticism and scholarly guidance are not really intelligible. But the study of the Old Testament as reinterpreted in our own generation by research and scholarship is a fascinating subject. It requires little in the way of technical equipment, and there is no reason in the world why it should be monopolized by specialists. To have even the most general acquaintance with the methods and results of critical study brings with it a great transformation of outlook. The Old Testament writers come to life again wonderfully when they are set in their proper historical context, and the result is a clear gain in spiritual values. The best general introduction to the whole subject is Dr. W. B. Selbie's book, The Nature and Message of the Bible (Student Christian Movement, 3s. 6d.). Canon Nairne's volume, The Faith of the Old Testament (Layman's Library, Longmans, 2s. 6d.) is an illuminating survey designed specially to bring out the religious value of the Old Testament, [10] and for commentaries upon individual books The Century Bible (T. C. and E. C. Jack, 3s. each volume) is to be recommended.

The books of the New Testament are the classical literature of Christianity in a much fuller and more obvious sense. Here, again, there is much that apart from the use of a good commentary will be found hardly intelligible: but the greater part of the New Testament, and especially the Gospels, can be read with profit by the ordinary man apart from any extraneous aids. It is well to remember that S. Paul's Epistles were written at an earlier date than any of the Gospels, and that they represent the occasional correspondence of a hard-worked missionary. Of the Gospels the first three have much in common, and the Gospels of S. Matthew and S. Luke are based partly upon that of S. Mark. S. Mark is said to have been the companion of S. Peter, and is probably the author of the Gospel which bears his name. It may be taken to represent his reminiscences of S. Peter's preaching. The Gospel now known as that according to S. Matthew appears to be the work of a compiler who fitted into the framework of S. Mark's story a considerable amount of additional matter, drawn chiefly from a collection of "sayings of Jesus" which an early Christian writer declares to have been made by S. Matthew in Aramaic. S. Matthew's name, it is thought, was subsequently attached to the resulting document, since it contained a large preponderance of material derived from his book on our Lord's sayings. The name of the actual compiler of the first Gospel has not survived.

S. Luke's Gospel is a compilation made upon somewhat similar lines, and is based, in large measure, upon the same two sources: but the author's researches extended also more widely, and his Gospel contains a large proportion of matter peculiar to itself, which critics commonly regard as being of high historical value. The author of the book was a Greek doctor who attended

---

[10] Those who may desire a more detailed and comprehensive treatment of the literary problems of the Old Testament should consult G. B. Gray, A Critical Introduction to the Literature of the Old Testament (Duckworth, 2s. 6d.).

upon S. Paul, accompanying the latter in his travels, and writing the Acts of the Apostles as a second volume in continuation of his Gospel. The Acts is partly based upon a kind of diary which S. Luke kept of his experiences as S. Paul's companion and physician.

It is probable that both the first and the third of our four Gospels were in existence shortly before, or at the latest very shortly after, the destruction of Jerusalem by the Romans in the year 70 A.D. The second Gospel, since they both drew upon it, must be even earlier.

The Gospel according to S. John is of a somewhat later date, and bears a different character. It is reflective and meditative, and is penetrated throughout by a mystical symbolism. In many ways it suggests rather a spiritual interpretation of the significance of Jesus than a literal portrait of Him. Again, it is the product of a Greek rather than of a Jewish atmosphere, though its narrative presents so many touches of extraordinary vividness, and the author shows so exact a knowledge of Jewish institutions and conditions of life in Palestine, that it is difficult not to think that the book must have been written by a Jew who knew Judaism before its downfall. It is supposed that the writing dates from the closing years of the first century, and tradition declares that the author was S. John in old age at Ephesus. This statement is, however, in dispute, and the authorship of the Gospel is uncertain. In point of fact, it does not matter who the writer was. There is no one of the interpreters of Jesus who had drunk more deeply of His Spirit than had he: nor is there any of the books of the New Testament which brings Jesus closer to us than the Gospel according to S. John, or speaks home with greater power to the heart and affections of the simplest Christian.

Part II

The Practice of the Christian Religion

Chapter I

The Christian Aim

Christianity in practice means the dedication of life to the unselfish service of GOD and man, in the light of the ideals of Jesus Christ, and in the power of an inward spiritual life which is hid with Christ in GOD. The Christian, renouncing such merely worldly ideals as self- advancement, personal or family ambition, the accumulation of money, or the enjoyment, for their own sake, of the things which money can buy, is called to seek first and in all things GOD'S Kingdom and His righteousness, in the assurance that whatever may be really necessary for the advancement of this aim will in due course be added unto him.

He is not to expect to find the practice of his religion to be, in a worldly sense, profitable; and the practice of his religion is to cover the whole of life. The desperate attempt to combine the service of GOD with that of Mammon is therefore to be abandoned. If riches increase, he is not to set his heart upon them. If poverty be his lot, he is to embrace poverty as a bride. The aim and object of his life is not to be to get his own will done, but to discover what for him is the will of GOD, and to do it. He is to be the slave of GOD in Christ, a living instrument in the hands of Another, called to co-operate in a purpose not his own, though a purpose which he is to embrace, and to make his own, in a spirit of loyal sonship.

This means, among other things, that life is to be interpreted in terms of vocation. It means that for every man there is a "calling," a particular line of life which GOD intends him to follow, a specific piece of service to GOD and to his neighbour which he is called upon to render. The motto of a Christian's life is to be the motto of his Master—"My meat is to do the will of

Him that sent Me, and to accomplish His work." Gifts and capacities, aptitudes for any special work, are therefore "talents," to be used in accordance with the will and purpose of the Giver. Opportunities and endowments, whatsoever they may be, are opportunities and endowments for service.

It does not necessarily follow from this that a realization of the truth of Christianity, and an awakening to the claims of religion, will lead to any outward change or radical alteration in the general conception of a man's life-work. It may or it may not do so. There are indubitably cases in which a man is called upon to abandon his previous career—to forsake prospects, however promising, or to renounce wealth and possessions, however entangling—in order to become (for example) a minister of the Church or a missionary of the Gospel, or to enter a religious order. Our Lord's command to the rich young ruler, that he should give up all that he had, in order to follow Christ along the paths of homelessness and poverty, is a call which sounds still with a literal force in the ears of a certain number of His disciples. The inner spirit, moreover, of detachment from the world and from the things of the world, the readiness to abandon wealth and worldly position if need so require, and the refusal to be ensnared by them, are in any case demanded of all. The vocation, however, of the majority of men is already determined by their circumstances, or by their training and general aptitudes. It is only the few, comparatively speaking, who are called to become monks or missionaries, or priests devoid of "prospects." The majority will best serve GOD and their neighbour by "carrying on" in their existing occupations: and in most cases they are incidentally called also, sooner or later, to matrimony.

But GOD calls no man to idleness. It is the duty of every Christian, rich as well as poor, unless he be incapacitated by bodily sickness or infirmity, to be engaged in some work of general service to the community: and a man who proposes seriously to practise the Christian religion needs to ask himself, with regard to the work or occupation in which he is engaged, or by which he earns his bread, whether he can say truly that he

70

believes it to be the work which his Father has given him to do: whether it can be interpreted, not simply as a means of livelihood, but as a service rendered in Christ's name to society at large. If it cannot so be interpreted, then plainly it is no work which a Christian should be doing. There are ways of making a living which, are definitely unchristian. The work of a shoe-black or of a tradesman or of an actor may be as true a piece of Christian service as that of a doctor or a bishop. The work of a burglar or of a bookmaker could not be so regarded.

Christianity—it cannot be too strongly insisted—means the Christianization of life as a whole. It is in the daily round and the common task that Christ is most chiefly to be served. "Whatsoever ye do in word or in deed, do all in the name of the Lord Jesus, giving thanks to GOD and the Father by Him." Religion is a wider thing than piety, and it is a false pietism which would regard it as consisting mainly of pious practices. The cultivation of the inner spiritual life by means of the practices of Christian devotion is indeed essential in its place and its degree. The life of the spirit languishes if it is not fed. But except these things issue in the practical service of Christ in daily life they are worse than futile. They degenerate either into formalism and hypocrisy, or into spiritual self- indulgence. "Herein is My Father glorified, that ye bear much fruit." "By their fruits ye shall know them." And the "fruits" of Christian living are to be discovered, not in the hours spent in devotion, but in the manifestation amid the activities of the market-place of that temper of righteousness and peace and joy in the Holy Ghost, and that spirit of unselfish service, which should be their normal product.

What is needed is a wider conception of Churchmanship and a truer doctrine of vocation. All honest work in which a Christian can lawfully engage should be regarded as an expression of his Churchmanship—as truly work done for the Church of GOD in obedience to a vocation from on high as is the work of a priest or a teacher of religion. It is at least partly because the majority of laymen do not so interpret their work in life that in so many cases they are discovered to be in effect living for the sake of their leisure and regarding their daily work as uninteresting drudgery, with the result that life as a whole comes to be for them dreary and profitless and stale. A Christian man's life-work ought not to have the character of drudgery, but of sheer delight in GOD'S service.

But is such an ideal really practicable? It is literally practicable to a greater extent than most men think. It ought to be practicable universally. At the same time there is no disguising the fact that large numbers of men to-day find themselves in circumstances to which such a doctrine cannot without palpable unreality be applied. The structure of existing society under modern industrial conditions forces multitudes, by an evil economic pressure, into mechanical, uncongenial, and soul-destroying occupations: and the conditions of some men's labour in the world as it is are such that it would be sheer blasphemy to regard them as a product of the will of GOD. The problem of the Christianization of the social order is one of the greatest of the tasks confronting the Christian Church. Its solution has hardly yet begun to be attempted. In the meantime the mass of Christian people, in virtue of their acquiescence, are accomplices in the denial to the disinherited classes of the conditions and opportunities which make life worth living for themselves. So long as it continues to be possible for a man who genuinely desires to learn and labour truly to get his own living to starve in the midst of plenty: so long as multitudes are constrained to work under conditions which rob their labour of all interest, of all idealism, and of all hope: so long as sweating, and destitution, and such conditions of life as obtain in the more densely crowded areas of our great towns continue to exist: so long will it be the duty of every Christian to be a social reformer, and to have a conscience permanently troubled with regard to wealth and social advantage.[11]

Meanwhile the Christian ideal of life stands. It is the ideal of consecration to service. It means discipleship in Christ's school of

___

[11] Mr. George Lansbury's Your Part in Poverty (George Allen and Unwin, Ltd., Is.) is a book worth reading in this particular connexion.

unselfishness, both individual and corporate: for there is a selfishness of the family, of the class, or of the nation, which bears as bitter fruit in the world as does the selfishness of the individual. Christianity, in a word, means the carrying out into daily practice of the ideal of the Imitatio Christi, the imitation of Jesus Christ, in the spirit if not in the letter. It means that as He was, so are we to be in the world. It means that all things, whatsoever we do, are to be done in His Spirit and to His glory: that our every thought is to be led captive under the obedience of Christ. It means that we are to love GOD because GOD first loved us, and to love men because they are our brothers in the family of GOD: because love is of GOD, and every one that loveth is born of GOD and knoweth GOD. It means that we are to consecrate all comradeship and loyalty and friendship, all sorrow and all joy, by looking upon them as friendship and loyalty and comradeship in Christ, as sorrow and joy in Him. It means that we are to live glad, strong, free, clean lives as sons of GOD in our Father's House.

It means also struggle and hardship. It means truceless war against the spirit of selfishness, against everything that tends to drag us down, against the law of sin in our own members. It means a truceless war against low ideals and tolerated evils in the world about us. It means soldiership in the eternal crusade of Christ against whatsoever things are false and dishonest and unjust and foul and ugly and of evil report.

It is an ideal which, considered in isolation from the Christian Gospel of redemption and the power of the Holy Spirit, could only terrify and daunt a man who had a spark of honesty in his composition: and for this reason the mass of men refuses to take it seriously. It is an ideal which, in the case of all who do take it seriously, convinces them of sin.

Nevertheless to lower the ideal, to abate one jot of its severity, to compromise, on the score of human weakness, though it were but in a single particular, the flawless perfection of its standard, were to prove false to all that is highest within us, and traitor to the cause of Christ.

"Never, O Christ—so stay me from relenting—Shall there be truce betwixt my flesh and soul."

Chapter II

The Way of the World

The three traditional enemies of the Christian life are symbolized under the headings of the World, the Flesh, and the Devil, and the classification has a certain convenience. The "World" stands in this connexion for human society in so far as it is organized apart from Christ. It is obvious that "the way of the world," as represented by the general outlook of conventional society, is in many respects in manifest conflict with the principles of the Gospel. The existing social order is the product of a compromise between inherited influences and standards which are in a certain sense broadly Christian, and the natural man's instinctive selfishness in matters both individual and social. The conflict against the spirit of worldliness which should be one of the marks of a genuine Christian life is beset by peculiar difficulties, precisely because in a society which is in some respects partially Christian the issues are confused. Public opinion indubitably tolerates many things which should not be tolerated, and condones others which should not be condoned. But public opinion approves much that is good, and does lip-service to a variety of Christian ideals, even while reserving the reality of its devotion for the worship of success and material comfort.

Perhaps it may be said that the most fundamental characteristic of essentially "worldly" opinion is absence of idealism. Worldliness is the principle of contentment with things as they are. Against worldliness, so defined, the Christian is committed to a conflict all along the line, since even in those regions of life and conduct in which the standards recognized by the world are right and good so far as they go, "the good is the enemy of the best." To rest content at any point with what has already been attained is fatal to all spiritual advance. It is, in effect, the death of the soul.

Mr. William Temple has remarked that in the conflict of Christians against the Devil and the Flesh the public opinion of the Church, as visibly organized, is on their side, but that in their conflict with the World it is decidedly against them. That is an over-statement, but it conveys a truth. Undoubtedly the Church has made compromises with the World, a fact which arises partly as the result of the inclusion within her fold of a large proportion of merely nominal members whose Christianity is no more than an inherited or conventional tradition. A further point of importance is this. Two thousand years is not a long period in relation to the scale of the world's history as a whole, and Christianity is still a comparatively young religion. The problem of worldliness is mainly a problem of the relation of the Church to the social order; and there are reasons why it was natural that the working out of the Christian ideal of conduct should first have been developed in relation to the affairs of private and domestic life.

Christians in the early days were a "little flock," surrounded by a society whose standards and conventions and beliefs were frankly pagan and hostile. So long as these conditions obtained the issues were plain: the contrast in ideals between Church and World stood out sharp and clear. The world, it was held, was ready to perish, and destined at no distant date to do so. "The whole world," writes S. John, "lieth in wickedness." The Church stood apart as the spiritual brotherhood of GOD'S elect who were called to assist at the obsequies of a world which was in process of passing away. "The world passeth away, and the lust thereof: but he that doeth the will of GOD abideth for ever."

The words contain an eternal truth: but in their literal sense they expressed a mistaken judgment. The world—that is, secular society— did not pass away. It is with us still. For a period of some three hundred years it persecuted the Church. At the end of that period it accepted baptism, but not its implications. The Church has been engaged ever since in the task of attempting to Christianize the heathen within her own borders.

The Church was outwardly secularized: and the minority who could not tolerate the secularization of her ideals took refuge in the hermit's cell or in the cloister. In these retreats was developed the practice of Christianity as an art or science of individual sanctity, but at the cost of a certain aloofness from the rough and tumble of workaday life. The Christianity of the Middle Ages was fertilized from the cloister, with the result that the spiritual ideals even of those Christians who remained "in the world" tended to be coloured by the monastic tradition. The Christian man of the world who took seriously the practice of his religion aimed at reproducing at second hand the Christianity of the monk. The salvation of the individual soul tended to be regarded as the supreme end of Christian endeavour, rather than the service of the brethren.

The Reformation, when it came, did nothing to diminish this individualism of the religious outlook, but rather accentuated it. The whole emphasis of Protestantism was thrown upon the life of the individual soul in relation to GOD, to the comparative neglect of the importance of the conception of membership in the Church. To the ordinary worldling the advent of Protestantism meant simply that he need no longer trouble to go to Mass or to Confession. The Protestant who took his religion seriously became a Puritan, a type resembling the monk of Catholicism in his attempted isolation from the world, yet lacking the peculiar otherworldly mysticism of the monkish character at its best, and having a peculiar knack of making religion appear repellent to the ordinary man.

The emergence of the ideal of a genuinely social Christianity, aiming not at escape from the world by way of flight, but at the deliberate conquest of the world for Christ by the resolute application of Christian standards to the ordinary life of men in society, is of comparatively recent date. It began in this country with the writings of Kingsley and Maurice, and various living teachers both in England and in America have carried on their work. It is one of the misfortunes of Germany that she has had no corresponding movement. As a consequence we are confronted at the present time with the spectacle of various leaders of religious thought in Germany, too honest not to perceive the glaring contrasts between the way of the world and the precepts of the

Gospel, deliberately maintaining the position that Christianity is solely adapted to be a religion of private life, and that Christian standards and ideals have no application as between class and class, or as between nation and nation. To adopt such an attitude is to abandon all hope of the redemption of society. It is to condemn the world in perpetuity to a fate of which the present war is the appropriate symbol.

The war is, in effect, a kind of sacrament of the power of Antichrist. It is the outward and visible sign of the inward character and essence of a civilisation founded upon principles which are the opposite of those of the Gospel. Neither men nor nations, in the world as we have known it, have been wont to love their neighbours as themselves. The way of the world is, and has been, the way of selfishness.

This is not any the less true because the world's selfishness has been to a considerable extent unconscious, and has arisen rather from absence of thought than from deliberate badness of heart. The world does not always realize how cruel are its ways towards the weak and the socially unfortunate, or towards those who, for whatever reason, transgress its code. For the world has a code of its own, both in manners and in morals, though the basis of its code is convention, and its standard respectability rather than virtue. The world is very apt to show itself implacable towards those whom it regards as being beyond its pale, and to exhibit, in effect, the spirit and temper which, when manifested in the religious sphere, we know and loathe as Pharisaism. Pharisaism, like worldliness, has penetrated to an alarming extent into the Church of England.

Parallel and proportionate to the world's selfishness is its cynicism. This also is largely unconscious. Lacking any true insight into spiritual realities, the world lacks vision and lacks hope. It presumes always that "the thing which has been, it is that which shall be." It beholds the evil that is done under the sun, and pronounces it inevitable. It fails to understand that to pronounce any evil inevitable is to be guilty of blasphemy against the GOD of heaven.

Against the spirit of the worldly world, its selfishness and cynicism, its conventional judgments and shallowness of mind, the Christian is called deliberately to make war. The Church exists to be to the world and its ways a permanent challenge: to be the champion in all circumstances and times of righteousness and truth; to insist upon bringing to bear on human life in all its relationships, both corporate and individual, the spirit of brotherhood, which is the Spirit of Christ. It was a true instinct which led S. Ignatius Loyola to pray on behalf of the Order which he founded that it might be hated by the world. "Marvel not, my brethren, if the world hate you.... If ye were of the world, the world would love his own." If the world does not hate the Church it is not because the world has become Christian, but because worldliness has taken possession of the Church. The world to-day regards the Church as not worth hating, as a negligible quantity. When the Church is once more ready to be crucified, then the opposition of the world will be revived, and the Church will suffer martyrdom afresh.

Chapter III

The Spirit and the Flesh

Sins of the flesh include all forms of slackness and bodily self- indulgence. A Christian is called to assert the supremacy of the spirit over the flesh by controlling his bodily impulses and disciplining his desires. There is, therefore, a true Christian asceticism. But asceticism, in so far as it is genuinely Christian, is never an end in itself. It is a discipline which promotes efficiency. It is to be compared to an athlete's training, not to the self-mutilation of a fakir. There is in Christianity no doctrine of the unlawfulness of bodily pleasures in themselves. "The Son of Man came eating and drinking." For Christianity every creature of GOD in itself is good, and a man's bodily impulses are God-given endowments of his nature. What is essential is that their exercise should be controlled and subordinated to the higher purposes of the spirit, that they should be directed to their proper ends, and that they should not be allowed to get out of hand. Christians are not meant to be Puritans, but they are meant to be pure. The battle against fleshliness in all its forms is a battle which has to be fought and won in every Christian's life.

Apart from the question of certain unmentionable forms of perverted sexual vice, the sinfulness of what are commonly classified as "sins of the flesh" consists in wrongful indulgence or lack of self-control in respect of that which in itself is legitimate and good. The Christian ideal is not abstinence, but temperance. A Christian will be temperate, for example, in sleep, food, alcohol, and tobacco. Intemperance means slavery to a habit, the loss of spiritual self- mastery, whereby the whole character is enervated, and efficiency, both physical and moral, is impaired. "All things are lawful," as S. Paul says, but a Christian is not to allow himself to be brought "under the power of any." He is meant to live hard and to live clean.

The practice of fasting, that is, of deliberate temporary self-discipline in these matters, even below the standard of what would normally be a reasonable indulgence, is a valuable means of asserting and retaining the self-mastery which is essential to Christian freedom. But fasting should not be allowed to become a mechanical observance, or erected into an unduly rigid law. The fish-dinner upon Fridays and other fast-days of the Church is, as a modern dignitary has remarked, innocuous; and it has the value which belongs to conformity to a rule or recommendation of the Christian brotherhood; but whether or not it is observed in practice, it is hardly adequate by itself to the purposes of Christian self-discipline.

It appears to be a fairly widespread delusion in some sections of society that a Christian must necessarily be a teetotaller. The ideal Christian policy, here as elsewhere, if we may judge from the example of our Lord, would seem to be that of a temperate use of the gifts of GOD. It is unfortunate that in this country most of the societies which exist for the purpose of promoting temperance have virtually committed themselves to the confusion of temperance with total abstinence, and their fanaticism is, in the judgment of many persons, a hindrance to genuine reform. But it cannot reasonably be denied that drunkenness, and the still wider prevalence of an excessive drinking which falls short of actual drunkenness, is a frightful evil in the national life; and what is commonly known as the "Liquor Interest" plays a sinister part as an organized obstructive force standing in the way of needed reforms. The number of public-houses and drinking- bars in English towns and villages is monstrously out of proportion to any reasonable needs of the population: and it must be more than ordinarily difficult for brewers and publicans, under existing conditions, to resist the temptation to exploit for the sake of gain the weaknesses of others. A Christian need not be a teetotaller in order to have this problem upon his conscience, and to be ready to support, by his vote and influence, some considered and constructive policy of reform. A man who by experience finds that alcohol is to him personally a temptation will be wise if he becomes a teetotaller. "If thy hand or thy foot offend thee, cut it off." In certain social environments it may also be wise for a man to become a total abstainer, not in his own interests, but for the sake of others with whom he is brought into immediate contact. There can be no question but that drunkenness, which is a vice both degrading and repulsive in itself, is in many strata of English social life still far too lightly regarded.

It is, moreover, worth remarking that even a degree of indulgence in alcohol which would commonly be regarded as falling well within the limit of temperance is regarded by some authorities as having the effect—which actual drunkenness certainly has—of stimulating sexuality: and when all is said, probably the most insistent of fleshly temptations, at least in the earlier years of manhood, are those which are connected with the life of sex. Many make shipwreck upon these rocks through lack of knowledge or want of thought; but neither thought nor knowledge will avail to safeguard a man's purity apart from sound moral principle: nor are even moral principles effectual in the hour of strong temptation apart from the grace of GOD.

Christianity teaches that to every man there is entrusted, in virtue of his manhood, the seed of life as a divine treasure. It is meant not to be turned into a means of self-indulgence, or suffered to run riot in a blaze of passion, but to be restrained and safeguarded in purity against the day—if the day arrives—upon which a man is called to use it for the purpose for which it was given him, namely, that of bringing new lives into the world through union with a woman in pure marriage.

Most men are sorely tempted to lack of self-control, and to the misuse of their sexual endowment in a variety of ways: and the maintenance of chastity—never an easy ideal—is made doubly difficult by the fact that in the existing social system marriage, except among the poorer classes, is commonly deferred until an age much later than that at which a man becomes physically mature, and also by the widespread prevalence, in masculine society, of a corrupt public opinion which regards sexual indulgence as morally tolerable, or even as essential to physical health. This latter doctrine, even were it as true as it is in fact false, would not in any case justify a man in taking advantage of a woman's ruin: but experience shows that there is no form of sin or indulgence which so effectually degrades a man's moral outlook, blunts his finer perceptions, and destroys the instinct of chivalry within him, as does the sin of fornication. The majority of those who practise promiscuous sexual intercourse are found to greet with frank and obviously genuine incredulity the assertion that there exists a not inconsiderable proportion of men whose lives are clean; while at the other end of the scale men of pure lives and clean ideals often find it difficult to believe that more than a small minority of peculiarly degraded individuals are clients of the women of the streets.

The publication of the Report of the Royal Commission on Venereal Diseases, taken in conjunction with what is known or suspected with regard to the state of morals in the Army, has had the effect of drawing public attention to certain aspects of these problems. The Victorian convention of prudery has to a great extent been discarded. The subject is freely discussed, and it is generally acknowledged that something must be done. There is danger, however, lest public opinion, rightly concerned to promote measures for the eradication of disease, should ignore the essentially moral aspect of the matter. A Christian man is here concerned, not simply with the personal struggle against the temptations of sex in his own life, but with a further conflict on behalf of Christian ideals against the public opinion of the world.

For if ecclesiastical opinion in the past has been both prudish and Pharisaic, the public opinion of the world is frankly cynical. Roughly speaking, the world expects the majority of women to be pure, acquiesces in the prostitution of the remainder, and treats masculine immorality as a venial offence. Numbers of would-be reformers—of the male sex—are not ashamed to advocate, in private if not in public, the establishment of licensed brothels on the continental model. It ought not to be necessary to say that no Christian man can possibly tolerate a proposal to give deliberate public sanction to the prostitution of a certain proportion of the nation's womanhood to the lusts of men, or acquiesce in the complacent sex-selfishness which is concerned only for the physical health of sinners of the male sex.

The point of view of the Christian Church is determined by that of our Lord, who on the one hand numbered a reclaimed prostitute among His intimate friends, and on the other taught that whoso looketh on a woman to lust after her hath committed adultery already in his heart. The Church, therefore, differs from the world, first in holding that what is wrong for women is equally wrong for men, that there is one and the same standard in these matters for both sexes, namely, absolute sexual purity; and secondly, in extending equally to the fallen of both sexes the promise of Divine forgiveness upon identical terms, namely, genuine repentance, unreserved confession, desire and purpose of amendment, and faith in GOD. The world, which condones the iniquity of the man who falls, is apt to be uncommonly hard upon the fallen woman, forgetting that she also is a sister for whom Christ died, and that the woman who to-day plays the part of a temptress of men was originally, in the majority of cases, more sinned against than sinning. Very few of those who ply the trade of shame will be found to have adopted such a mode of life, in the first instance, of their own unfettered choice. We are members one of another, and society as a whole, which both creates the demand and provides the supply, must share the guilt of their downfall.

This book is written primarily for men: and there are therefore other aspects of the life of sex upon which it is necessary to touch, though they are difficult matters to handle. It is well known that large numbers of men in boyhood, either through untutored ignorance of the physiology of their own bodies, or as a result of the corrupt example and teaching of others, become addicted to habits of solitary vice, in which the seed of life within them is deliberately excited, stirred up and wasted, to the sapping of their physical well-being and the defilement of their minds. Habits of self-abuse, when once they are established, are apt to be extremely difficult to break. The minds of their victims are liable to be morbidly obsessed by the physical facts of sex, and their thoughts continually directed into turbid channels. But it is possible by the grace of GOD to conquer, though there may be relapses before the final victory is won. It is important neither on the one hand to belittle the gravity of the evil, nor on the other to grow hopeless and despondent, but to have faith in GOD. It is also a counsel of common sense to distract the mind, so far as possible, in other directions, and to avoid deliberately whatever is likely to prove an occasion or stimulus to this particular form of sin. The battle of purity can only be successfully fought in the region of outward act if the victory is at the same time won in the region of thought and desire. Books and pictures, or trains of thought and imagination, which are either unclean in themselves, or are discovered by experience to be sexually exciting to particular individuals, ought obviously to be avoided by those concerned, and the mind directed towards the contemplation of whatsoever things are true and honest and just and pure and lovely and of good report. In the hour of strong temptation it is often best, instead of trying to meet the assault directly, to change the immediate environment, or in some other way to concentrate the mind: for example, to sit down and read a clean novel until the stress of the obsession is past. Physical cleanliness, plenty of healthy exercise in the open air (it is unfortunate that the circumstances of many men's lives do not give adequate opportunity for this), temperance in food, and especially—in the light of what has been said above—temperance in drink, are all incidentally of value as aids to the maintenance of purity. So also is the avoidance of the habit of lying in bed in a semi-somnolent condition after true sleep has finally departed. A Christian's body is meant to be a temple of the Holy Ghost, and no other spirit, whether of impurity or of sloth, should be allowed to have domination over him.

Other sins there are which should not be so much as named among Christian men-those, namely, in which men with men work that which is unseemly, and burn with lust one towards another. It is necessary to refer to these, because their prevalence is said to be increasing. A considerable proportion of men are temperamentally liable to be sexually attracted by members of their own sex; and passionate friendships, in which there is an element which is in the last analysis sexual, are not uncommon both between boys and youths at the age of early manhood, and between men of mature age and adolescents. The true character of these relationships is not always in their initial stages obvious, even to those concerned. As a guiding principle it may be laid down that a friendship between members of the same sex begins to enter upon dangerous ground whenever an element of jealousy betrays itself, when there is a desire habitually to monopolize the other's company to the exclusion of third persons, or when the life and interests of the one appear to be disproportionately wrapped up in the concerns and doings of the other. Friendships of this character are always selfish and may all too easily become impure. It is the business of a Christian man to be on his guard and to love his male friends not as a woman is loved and not in a spirit of selfish monopoly, but with the pure and clean and essentially unselfish affection of Christian manhood.

A word may be said, lastly, with regard to prurient and polluted talk and unclean stories. Against these a Christian man will do well firmly and resolutely to set his face. Such things defile the mind. They are injurious both to him that hears and to him that speaks, in that they tend to engender a mental atmosphere in which the suggestions of actual vice are likely to meet with an enfeebled power of resistance. Of course it is possible to be too tragical on the subject of "language," and to exaggerate the harm done by "smoking-room" stories. But whatever is definitely unclean is definitely evil, and should be both avoided and discouraged. To assume, however, a pious demeanour and to appear to be shocked is a fatal method of protest. Christians have no business to be shocked, nor are they meant to be prigs. There are other forms of social pressure which are more effective. It is, moreover, sometimes possible to combine moral reprobation with a sense of humour.

Chapter IV

The Works of the Devil

The devil is from one point of view a figure of Jewish and Christian mythology. The Jews, like other early peoples, believed in the existence of evil spirits or demons, to whose malignant agency they ascribed various diseases, both functional and organic, and in particular those unhappy cases of obsession, fixed idea, and multiple personality, which we should now class under the general head of insanity, and treat in asylums for the mentally deranged. The New Testament writings are full of this point of view, which is of course largely foreign to our minds to-day. The ordinary Englishman is not a great believer in devils or spirits of evil: though he does in some instances believe in ghosts, and is inclined to the practice of what in former ages was called necromancy—the attempt to establish an illicit connexion with the spirits of the departed—under the modern name of psychical research. There are, no doubt, some forms of psychical research which are genuinely scientific and legitimate. It is probable enough that there exists a considerable area of what may be called borderland phenomena to which scientific methods of inquiry may be found applicable, and which it is theoretically the business of science to investigate. But it is a region in which the way lies readily open to all kinds of superstition and self-deceit. The pursuit of truth for its own sake is essentially a religious thing: but the motives of many amateur dabblers in psychical research are far from being truly religious or spiritual. Much popular spiritualism, whether it assumes the form of table-turnings, of spirit-rappings, or of mediumistic seances, is thoroughly morbid and undesirable, and the Christian Church has rightly discouraged it.

It is not, however, necessary to believe literally in the devil, or in devils—concerning whose existence many persons will prefer to remain agnostic—in order to find in the figure of the devil, as he appears in Biblical and other literature, a convenient personification of certain forms of evil. There is an atmosphere of evil about us, a Kingdom of Evil, over against the Kingdom of Good: and there are suggestions and impulses of evil which from time to time arise in our minds, which–whatever may be the literal truth about them–not infrequently present the appearance of having been prompted by some mysterious external Tempter. Certainly deeds have been done in the present war which can only be described as devilish. The war has revealed on a large scale and in unmistakable terms the evil of which the heart of man is capable, and how thin in many cases is the veneer which separates the outwardly civilized European from the primitive savage. "For this purpose was the Son of GOD manifested, that He might destroy the works of the devil." And by the works of the devil we may understand especially cruelty, malice, envy, hatred and all uncharitableness, the spirit of selfishness which wars against love, and the spirit of pride which ignores GOD. We see these things exhibited upon the large scale in the conspicuous criminals among mankind, whom we are sometimes tempted to regard as devils incarnate. We need to be on our guard against the beginnings of them, and indeed in many cases their actual presence in an undetected but fairly developed form, in ourselves.

(i) Christian men are to be kindly affectioned one towards another in brotherly love: in honour preferring one another–which is easier to say than to do. They are to refrain from rendering evil for evil, and to learn under provocation to be self-controlled. They are to be in charity with all men, and so far as it lies within their own power (for it takes two to make peace, as it takes two to make a quarrel) they are to live peaceably with all men. Wrath and clamour, lying and evil-speaking, back-biting and slandering, are all of the devil, devilish. Contrary to the works of the devil, which may be summed up under the three headings of lying, hatred, and pride, are the Christian ideals of truthfulness, love, and humility, with regard to each of which a few words may usefully be said.

(i) The devil is described in the New Testament as "a liar and the father thereof." A Christian is to be true and just in all his dealings, abhorring crookedness: for the essence of lying is not

88

inexactitude in speech, but deceitfulness of intention. Christian veracity means honesty, straightforwardness, and sincerity in deed as well as in word. A writer of fiction is not a liar: to improve in the telling an anecdote or a story is not necessarily to deceive others in any culpable sense; and moralists have from time to time discussed the question whether there may not be circumstances in which to tell a verbal lie is even a moral duty—e.g. in order to prevent a murderer or a madman from discovering the whereabouts of his intended victim. But casuistical problems of this kind do not very frequently arise, and in all ordinary circumstances strict literal veracity is the right course to pursue. [12]

Christian truthfulness, however, is in any case a much wider thing than merely verbal truth-telling: it implies inward spiritual reality, a genuine desire to see things as they are, a thirst of the soul for truth, and a hatred of shams. The worst form of lying is that in which a man is not merely a deceiver of others but is self-deceived, and suffers from "the lie in the soul." The religion of Christ is always remorselessly opposed to every form or kind of humbug or of sham. Jesus Christ is the supreme spiritual realist of history. In His view the "publican" or acknowledged sinner is preferable to the Pharisee or hypocrite for the precise reason that the former is a more genuine kind of person than the latter. And to tell the truth in this deeper sense, that is, genuinely to face realities and to refuse to be put off with shams, to see through the plausibilities and to detect the hollowness of moral and social pretences and conventionalities, to have, in short, the spiritual and moral instinct for reality, is a much harder thing than to be verbally veracious. The true veracity can come only from Him who is the Truth: it is a gift of the Spirit, and proceeds from GOD who knows the counsels of men's hearts, and discerns the motives and imaginations of their minds.

---

[12] Of course such social conventions as "Not at home," "No trouble at all," or "Glad to see you," "No, you are not interrupting me," etc., are hardly to be classed as "lies," since they do not as a rule seriously mislead others, but are merely an expression of the will to be civil.

It follows that just as every lie is of the devil, so all truth, of whatever kind, is of GOD. The Lord is a God of Knowledge, and every form of intellectual timidity and obscurantism is contrary to godliness. There can never be any opposition between scientific and religious truth, since both equally proceed from GOD. The Christian Church is ideally a society of free-thinkers, that is, of men who freely think, and the genuine Christian tradition has always been to promote learning and freedom of inquiry. It is worth remembering that the oldest and most justly venerable of the Universities of Europe are without exception in their origin ecclesiastical foundations. If the love of truth and the spirit of freedom which inspired their inception has at particular epochs in their history been temporarily obscured, if there is much in the ecclesiasticism both of the past and of the present which is reactionary in tendency and spirit, at least there have never been lacking protesting voices, and the authentic spirit of the Gospel tells always upon the other side. "Ye shall know the truth," says a New Testament writer, "and the truth shall make you free." [13]

(ii) In the second place, hatred is of the devil, and love is of Christ: the Christian is to love even his enemies. In a time of war, that is to say, whenever actual enemies exist, the natural man discovers in such an ideal only an immoral sentimentalism, and the doctrinaire pacificist occasionally uses language which gives colour to the charge. But Christianity has nothing in common with sentimentalism, and Christian is no merely sentimental affection which ignores the reality of evil or explains away the wrongfulness of wrong. In order to love his enemies it is not necessary for a Christian to pretend that they are not really hostile, to make excuses for things that are inexcusable, or to be blind to

---

[13] The manifestations of the persecuting spirit and temper are not confined to the sphere of religion; the intolerance of the platform or of the press can be as bigoted as that of the pulpit: and secular governments also can persecute—not only in France or in Prussia. That it is part of the mission of Christianity to cast out the evil spirit of persecution, to destroy intolerance as it has destroyed slavery, is none the less true, in spite of the fact that both slavery and persecution have in the past found Christian defenders.

the moral issues which may be at stake. It has rightly been pointed out that "Love your enemies" means "Want them to be your friends: want them to alter, so that friendship between you and them may become possible." More generally what is meant is that the Christian man is by the grace of GOD, to conquer the instinct of hatred and the spirit of revenge within his own heart, to be willing to serve others (his enemies included) at cost to himself in accordance with the will of GOD, to desire on behalf of all men (his enemies included) the realization of their true good. For wrongdoers chastisement may be the truest kindness. To allow a man, or a nation, to pursue an evil purpose unchecked would be no real act of love even towards the nation or the individual concerned. To offer opposition, if necessary by force, may in certain circumstances be a plain duty. That which we are to love, in those whose immediate aspect and character is both unlovely and unlovable, is not what they are, but what they are capable of becoming. We are to love that element in them which is capable of redemption, the true spiritual image of GOD in man, which can never be totally effaced. We are to remember that for them also the Son of GOD was crucified, that we also have need of forgiveness, and that "GOD commendeth His own love towards us, in that, while we were yet sinners, in due time Christ died for the ungodly."

(iii) The third great manifestation of the spirit and temper which is of the devil, devilish, is pride, which by Christian writers upon these subjects is commonly regarded as the deadliest of the so-called "deadly sins," on the ground that it logically involves the assertion of a false claim to be independent of GOD, and is therefore fatal in principle to the religious life. Pagan systems of morality distinguish between false pride, the foolish conceit of the man who claims for himself virtues and capacities which he does not in fact possess, and proper pride, the entirely just appreciation by a man of his own merits and accomplishments at neither more nor less than their true value. The Christian ideal of humility is apt from this point of view to appear either slavish or insincere. The issue between Christian and pagan morals here depends upon the truth or falsehood of the Christian doctrine of GOD and of His relation to man. Once let a man take seriously the avowal that "It is He that hath made us, and not we ourselves," once let him grant the position that his life belongs to GOD and not to himself, and concur in the judgment of spiritual experience that whatever is good in him is the result not of his own efforts in independence of his Maker, but of the Divine Spirit operative within him, and it becomes obvious that "boasting"—as S. Paul expresses it—"is excluded."

At the same time Christian humility is not self-depreciation. It has nothing in common either with the spirit of Uriah Heep, or with the false diffidence which refuses on the ground of personal insufficiency a task or vocation to which a man is genuinely called. These are both equally forms of self-consciousness. Humility is forgetfulness of self. The true pattern and exemplar of humility is the Christ, who claimed for Himself the greatest role in the whole history of the world, simply on the ground that it was the work which His Father had given Him to do. "I seek not Mine own glory: there is One that seeketh and judgeth." The secret of humility is devotion to the will of GOD.

Chapter V

The Kingdom of God

Christianity in the last three chapters has been considered on its negative side as involving a conflict against temptation. But the Christian ideal is positive rather than negative. We have only to think for a moment of the character and life of Christ in order to realize how ludicrously impoverished a conception of the Gospel righteousness is that which regards it as exhausted by the meticulous avoidance of sin. "Christian purity," it has been said, "is not a snowy abstinence but a white-hot passion of life towards GOD." The same might be said of other Christian virtues. Positively regarded, the Christian ideal of life means sonship towards GOD and citizenship in His Kingdom.

The precise signification of the phrase, "Kingdom of GOD," or "Kingdom of Heaven," in the language of the New Testament has been the theme of controversy and discussion among scholars. It is impossible to enter here into the technicalities of the dispute. Broadly speaking, it may be laid down without much fear of contradiction that the Kingdom of GOD means the effectual realization, in every department of human life and upon a universal scale, of the sovereignty of GOD as Christ reveals Him. It is the vision of the goal of human history. It is meant to be a leading motive and inspiration of Christian life.

> "I will not cease from mental strife,
>   Nor shall my sword sleep in my hand,
>   Till we have built Jerusalem
>   In England's green and pleasant land."

It is quite true that, according to the thought of the New Testament writers, the mystic Jerusalem is not a city built by mortal men upon this earth, but something which is wholly the gift of GOD, a city not made with hands, descending from GOD out of heaven. The Kingdom of GOD in its fulness is no product of human striving. It is the achievement of a Divine purpose, the manifestation in the end of the days of the completed mystery of the Divine Will.

Nevertheless it is the mission of the Church to prepare the way of the Kingdom, and it is for Christian men to live as sons of the Divine Kingdom even now, that is, as men in whose hearts and lives GOD and none other is enthroned as King and Lord. This means that everything that is good in human life is to be redeemed by being offered to GOD, and that everything that is vile and evil is to be eliminated and cast out. "The Son of Man shall send forth His messengers, and they shall gather out of His Kingdom all things that offend." "There shall in no wise enter into it anything that defileth, neither whatsoever worketh abomination, or maketh a lie." "The Kingdom of GOD is righteousness and peace and joy in the Holy Ghost."

The ideal of the Christian life, therefore, is something infinitely richer and more positive than the merely negative morality of the Ten Commandments. It is the ideal of the Divine Kingdom. It is a positive devotion to the will of GOD. It means co-operation with the Divine will and purpose, a will and a purpose which, by the patient operation of the Divine Spirit, is in the course of world-history slowly but surely being worked out, amid all the immediate chaos and welter of events, to its goal in the revelation of the Jerusalem which is from above. That is why the Christian is bidden to pray continually, "Thy Kingdom come, Thy will be done, in earth as it is in heaven."

If a man does not want the Divine Kingdom, or does not believe in it, he ought not to pray for it. If he does want it and pray for it, he ought also to work for it. And though no man may fully understand it, yet if a man is to pray for it and work for it at all, he needs to have at least some partial understanding of what it means. It is worth while, therefore, instead of dismissing the idea as a vague dream or an empty phrase, to try and fill it with some measure of positive meaning for us men here and now. What is the will of GOD for humanity? And what is meant by preparing the way of the Lord? Some things at least we may say are certainly included in the will of GOD, and some things are as certainly excluded.

"It is not the will of your Father which is in heaven that one of these little ones should perish." A Christian Church which took seriously its vocation to go before the Lord and to prepare His ways would be effectively and vigorously concerned with problems so prosaic as the rate of infantile mortality and the allied questions of housing and sanitation, with the insistence that the conditions of life among the poorer classes of the community shall be such as make decent living possible, and with the provision of a minimum of leisure and of genuine opportunities of liberal education for all who have the will and the capacity to profit by them. The combined ignorance and apathy of the people of England with regard to questions of education, which has made possible the shelving of Mr. Fisher's Education Bill in deference to the opposition of vested interests, is little to the credit of the Christian Church in these islands, and grievously disappointing to those who had hoped at last for a real instalment of constructive reform. [14]

A system of education, moreover, which was truly Christian, would provide not merely for the training of mind and body, and for instruction—on the basis of some inter-denominational modus vivendi yet to be achieved—in morality and religion. It would secure equally for the children of all classes opportunities for the training of the aesthetic faculties, for the cultivation of art and imagination, for the filling of life with colour and variety and movement. The intolerable ugliness of the domestic architecture of our cities and towns is a totally unnecessary offence to GOD and man; and the drabness and monotony of the life of huge masses of the population, who find in the rival attractions of the

---

[14] It is now stated that the Bill is to be reintroduced and passed, with certain modifications. It is to be hoped that the modifications will not be such as to destroy its effectiveness as an instrument of real reform. It remains true that the Bill was imperilled by the apathy and ignorance of the rank and file of Churchmen and Christians generally, though it is fair to say that the Bishops demonstrated unanimously in its favour.

gin-palace and the cinema the only means of distraction at present open to them—this also is something which cannot possibly be regarded as being in accordance with the will of GOD. The redemption of society from all that at present makes human life sordid or hideous is a real part of what the ideal of the Kingdom means. It is a part of the task laid upon the Christian Church in preparing the way of the Lord and making straight His paths.

Included also in the will of GOD for humanity is the evangelization of the world, the perfecting of the Church, the bringing of all nations and races into a spiritual unity in Christ Jesus. Christianity claims by its very nature to be the absolute religion: the climax and fulfilment of the whole process of man's religious quest: the synthetic and unifying truth, in which whatever is true and positive and permanently valuable in the religious systems of the non-Christian world is gathered up and made complete. Of Christ it has been written that "How many soever be the promises of GOD, in Him is the yea." In Christ is the fulfilment of the unconscious prophecies of the religions of the heathen world, nor is there any true solution of the problems of comparative religion except this. The Christian Church is in principle and of necessity missionary, and apart from the vitalizing breath of the missionary spirit the life of the Church languishes and dies.

But the true spirit and method of Christian missions is not a narrow proselytism. There are indeed things in many of the lower religions of the world which are dark and evil. There are regions of the earth which are full of base and cruel and degrading superstitions, immoral rites and practices against which the Church of Christ can only set its face, and with which it can make no terms. These are works of the devil which the Son of GOD was manifested to destroy. But there is much in the higher religious thought of paganism which Christ comes not to destroy but to fulfil, and Christianity can fulfil and interpret to the higher religions of paganism just that which is truest and most positive in their own spiritual message. Conversely, it is probable that there are in Christianity itself elements which will only be fully interpreted and understood when the spiritual genius of nations at present pagan has made its proper contribution to Christian thought. For our own sake as well as for theirs it is important that the nations should be evangelized and brought to a knowledge of the truth. When we say the Lord's Prayer we are praying, among other things, for the success of Christian Missions.

And if Christianity contains within itself the true solution of the problem of comparative religion, it contains also, in germ and potentiality, the solution of the problems of race and caste, and of the international problem also. Not until men have learnt the secret of brotherhood in Christ will the white and the coloured races treat one another as brothers. Not until the nations, as nations, are genuinely Christian and have learnt, in their dealings one with another, to manifest the spirit of unselfishness and love, will the day be in sight when they shall beat their swords into ploughshares and be content to learn war no more. This too, if the Gospel means anything at all, is part of the will of GOD for the human race. It is part of what is involved in the prayer, "Thy will be done in earth, as it is in heaven." It is an integral and vitally important element in the Christian hope of the Kingdom.

The redemption of society, the evangelization of the world, the bringing together into the corporate wholeness of a world-wide Catholic Church of the fragmentary Christianity of the existing multitude of sects, the elimination of war from the earth, and the breaking down, as the result of a conscious realization of human unity in Christ, of the dividing barriers of colour and race and caste-all these are essential elements in the Christian vision. The man of the world may, and probably will, pronounce each and all of them to be chimerical, the baseless fabric of a dream. He will find no thoughtful man who is genuinely Christian to agree with him.

For these things are, quite certainly, part of the will of GOD for humanity. They are involved of necessity in any effectual realization in human life of the sovereignty of the Father who is revealed in Christ. And because GOD is GOD, the goal, for the Christian man, is within the horizon-"The Kingdom of heaven is at hand." In any case, be the goal near or be it far off, it is as a citizen of that Kingdom, and of none other, that the Christian man will set himself to live. He will enthrone GOD in his own heart as King and Lord, and will hold fast the heavenly vision which it has been given to him to see.

"As we look out into the future," says a modern writer,[15] "we seem to see a great army drawn from every nation under heaven, from every social class, from every section of Christ's Church, pledged to one thing and to one thing only-the establishment of Christ's Kingdom upon earth by His method of sacrifice and the application of His principle of brotherhood to every phase of human life. And as they labour there takes shape a world much like our own, and yet how different! Still individuals and communities, but the individual always serving the community and the community protecting the individual: still city and country life, with all their manifold pursuits, but no leading into captivity and no complaining in our streets: still Eastern and Western, but no grasping worldliness in the West, no deadening pessimism in the East: still richer and poorer, but no thoughtless luxury, no grinding destitution: still sorrow, but no bitterness: still failure, but no oppression: still priest and people, yet both alike unitedly presenting before the Eternal Father the one unceasing sacrifice for human life in body broken and blood shed: still Church and World, yet both together celebrating unintermittently the one Divine Service, which is the service of mankind. And in that climax of a vision, which, if we are faithful, shall be prophecy, what is it that has happened?

"'The kingdoms of this world have become the Kingdom of our GOD and of His Christ.'"

---

[15] The Rev. W. Temple, in an address delivered at Liverpool on "Problems of Society" in 1912, and published by the Student Christian Movement in Christ and, Human Need.

Chapter VI

Christianity and Commerce

This chapter ought properly to be written by a layman who
is also a Christian man of business. It is inserted here mainly to
challenge inquiry and to provoke thought. The writer has no first-
hand acquaintance either with business life or with business
methods. He desires simply to chronicle an impression that the
level of morality in the business world has been declining in
recent years, and that the more thoughtful and candid of
Christian laymen in business are beginning to be deeply
disquieted. It is not uncommon to be confronted by the statement
that it is impossible in modern business life to regulate conduct
by Christian standards. The impression exists that if large
numbers of business men abstain from the outward observances
of religion, it is in many cases because they are conscious of a lack
of correspondence between Sunday professions and weekday
practice, and have no desire to add hypocrisy to existing burdens
upon conscience. The clergy are by the circumstances of their
calling sheltered from the particular difficulties and temptations
which beset laymen in the business world. Their exhortations are
apt to sound in the ears of laymen abstract and remote from life.

If the situation has been diagnosed correctly the matter is
serious. What is suggested is not that men to-day are deliberately
more unprincipled than were their fathers, but that modern
conditions have made the way of righteousness more difficult.
Things have been speeded up. The competitive struggle has been
intensified. Men are beset, it has been said, by a "moral
powerlessness." They are "as good as they dare be." Absorbed in
money-making, and pressed hard by unscrupulous rivals, they
cannot afford to scrutinize too narrowly the social consequences
of what they do, or the strict morality of the methods which they
employ. Honesty, as experience demonstrates, is by no means
always the best policy from a worldly point of view. "The
children of this world are in their generation wiser than the

children of light." This being so, it is to be feared that men are apt to prefer the wisdom of the serpent to the harmlessness of the dove.

Moreover the man of business in the majority of cases does not stand alone. He is a breadwinner on behalf of others. Very commonly he regards it as a point of honour to refrain from disclosing to those at home his business perplexities and trials. It is assumed that they would not be understood, or that in any case it is unfair to burden wife and children with financial troubles. In the result it sometimes happens that a man's foes are found to be they of his own household, and that for the sake of wife and child he stoops to procedures which his own conscience condemns, and which those for whose sake he embarks upon them would be the first to disapprove. A wife, it may be suggested, ought to share the knowledge of her husband's difficulties, and to be willing, if need so require, to suffer loss and diminution of income as the price of her husband's honour. A wife takes her husband in matrimony "for poorer" as well as "for richer," for sickness and poverty as well as for health and wealth. It is a tragedy that in modern marriages too often only the more pleasurable alternative is seriously meant.

Enough has been said to make it evident that in the world of modern business there is a battle to be fought on behalf of Christ. Precisely for the reason that the vocation of a Christian in this sphere is in some ways the most difficult it is also the most necessary. There is a call for courage and consecration, for hard thinking and readiness for sacrifice, and from the nature of the case it must be mainly a laymen's battle. There may have to be financial martyrdoms for the sake of Christ before the victory is won. But the prize and the goal is worth striving for, for it is nothing less than the redemption of a large element in human life from the tyranny of selfishness and greed. [16]

---

[16] It may, of course, be argued that so long as the competitive system prevails in the business world, a Christian man in business must compete, just as in the existing state; though in an ideally Christian world competition would be replaced by co-operative and war would be unknown. This is perfectively true.

In principle the issues are clear enough. The interchange of commodities is a service rendered to the community. It ought to be so regarded, and the service rendered, rather than the gain secured, should be its inspiration and motive. The service of man is a form of the service of GOD, and the operations of financiers and business men ought to be capable of interpretation as forms of social service. It is only as this spirit is infused into the lives and practice of men in business that the world of business can be saved from degenerating into a soulless mechanism, dominated by the idea of purely selfish profit, or a tissue of dishonest speculation and sordid gambling. The business man, like any other servant of the community, is entitled to a living wage. He is not entitled either by chicanery and trickery, or by taking advantage of the needs of others and his own control of markets, to become a "profiteer." Profiteering in time of war is condemned by the common conscience. It is equally to be condemned in time of peace. The Christian man in business will stand for integrity and just dealing, for human sympathy and the spirit of service, for the renunciation of profits which are unreasonable and unfair. His function is not to exploit the community in his own personal or sectional interests, but to be a servant of the Christian commonwealth. Some procedures and some methods of making money the Christian man will feel himself debarred from employing. For the rest what is needed is mainly a change of heart, a shifting of emphasis, a modification of the inward spirit and motive of business life.

But it should be possible, nevertheless, to hold fast the Christian ideal as a regulative principle even under present conditions. Only in proportion as this is done is the redemption of business life a possibility.

Chapter VII

Christianity and Industry

Labour problems have always existed, but the development of industrialism as we know it to-day is comparatively modern. It dates from the introduction of machinery and mechanical transport, and coincided in its beginnings with the vogue of the so-called "Manchester School" in political and economic theory. The modern world of industry has been built up by the enterprise of capitalists working upon the basis of unrestricted competition. Joint-stock companies and "trusts" are simply capitalistic combinations for the exploitation of industrial opportunities upon a larger scale.

The economic theorists of the Manchester School regarded wages as necessarily governed by the working of the "iron law" of supply and demand. It was the "interest" of the employer to buy such labour as was required at as cheap a rate as possible. It was assumed that in this, as in other matters of "business," his procedure must be determined wholly by self-interest, to the exclusion of "sentimental" considerations. Individual employers might be better than their creed, and in the smaller "concerns" the relations between employer and employed were often humanized by personal knowledge and intercourse. With the advent of the joint-stock company this no longer held good. "A corporation has no bowels." Directors were not personally in contact with their workpeople, and their main consideration was for their shareholders. The whole tendency of the industrial order of society as it developed was in the direction of the exploitation of the workman in the interests of "capital."

It was not that members of the employing class were consciously inhuman. It was simply that they were blinded to the human problems which were involved. They had become accustomed to regard as natural and inevitable a wage-slavery of the many to the few. Labour was a commodity in the market. The workman was a unit of labour. Regarded from the point of view of Capital he represented simply the potentiality of so many foot-pounds of more or less intelligently- directed energy per diem. His life as a human being, apart from the economic value of his labour, was from the "business" point of view irrelevant.

The system was based upon a lie. "Treat human beings as machines as much as you will, the fact remains that they are incurably personal." The wage-slaves of the modern world asserted their personality, and the modern Socialist-Labour Movement is the result. The forces of organized labour have won some notable victories. They are a recognized power in the land. There are those who hope, and those who fear, that they will in the end become socially and politically omnipotent. It is now generally recognized that society prior to the war was on the brink of a struggle between the classes of great bitterness, and that the social condition of the country after the war is likely to be fraught with formidable possibilities. There are many observers who regard a social revolution, in one form or another, as inevitable.

Much, no doubt, will depend upon the temper of the returning troops, both officers and men. That men and officers have learnt to know and to respect one another upon the battlefield is acknowledged, but those who imagine that herein is contained a solution of social and labour problems are likely to prove grievously disappointed. A great deal of nonsense is being talked about the effects of "discipline" upon the men. Military discipline has its admirers: but men of mature years and civilian traditions who in the present conflict have served in the ranks of His Majesty's Army are not included among their number. They have submitted to discipline for the period of their military service. They are quite able to recognize that it is essential to the efficiency of the army as a fighting machine. But they conceive themselves to have been fighting for freedom: and their own freedom and that of their children and of their class is included in their eyes among the objects for which they fight. They will be more than ever jealous, after the war, of their recovered liberties, and determined to assert them. It is probable that one result of demobilization will be an enormous accession of strength to the ranks of the Socialist and Labour parties. The "class war" with which society was threatened before the European War broke out is not likely to be a less present danger when "that which now restraineth "is removed by the conclusion of peace.

What in relation to these problems is the message of the Christian Church? The distinctively Christian ethic is based not upon self- assertion but upon self-sacrifice, not upon class distinctions but upon brotherhood. "Let no man seek his own, but each his neighbour's good." The principle is of corporate as well as of individual application. In an ideally Christian society, the interests of "Labour" would be the sole concern of "Capital," the interests of "Capital" the sole concern of "Labour": and the message of the Church to the contending parties should be, now as always, "Sirs, ye are brethren."

Neither party, however, is likely at present to pay much heed to such a message, which is apt to sound like an abstract and theoretical truism remote from the actualities of life. In point of fact, the large sections of the population who live permanently near or below the poverty line are largely precluded by lack of leisure from entering into the Christian heritage of the spiritual life, and are too much obsessed by the daily struggle for material existence to have patience with exhortations to regard with sympathy either the temptations or the good intentions of the well-to-do. The latter in turn are apt to resent any attempt to stir in them a social conscience with regard to the problems of poverty or the fundamental causes of labour "unrest," to regard the security of dividends as conveniently guaranteed by the laws of GOD, and to hold, in a general way, that everything has hitherto been ordered for the best in the best of all possible worlds. The Church—and more particularly the Church of England—is commonly regarded both by "Labour" and by "Capital" as traditionally identified with the Conservative Party in politics. The Church-going classes love to have it so, and the world of Labour not unnaturally holds aloof.

It is nevertheless sufficiently obvious that the future of civilization after the war will be largely in the hands (or at the mercy) of organized Labour. And it is worth remembering that our Saviour died not for the rich only, but for the poor, having moreover Himself lived and worked as a labouring Man. There are those who regard the spirit of idealism and world-wide brotherhood by which the Labour Movement is inspired as the most profoundly Christian element in the life of the modern world, and the existing cleavage between Labour and the Church as a tragedy comparable only to the tragedy of the war. It is the plain duty of a Christian man to do what in him lies to remedy this cleavage, to think hard and honestly about social problems from a Christian point of view, and to make it his business to have an adequate understanding and sympathy with the real character and motives of Labour aspirations and ideals.

Chapter VIII

Christianity and Politics

Politics at their worst are a discreditable struggle between parties and groups for selfish, and sectional ends, full of dishonesty and chicanery and corruption. It is often recognized at the present time as desirable that none should be for party, but all for the state. The Christian ideal goes further than this: it is that none should be for party, but all for the Kingdom of GOD, and for the state only in so far as the state is capable of being made the instrument of that higher ideal. The Christian man is not to hold aloof from political life, but to seek, so far as his personal effort and influence can be made to tell, to Christianize the political struggle. In every contested election he is bound to think out in the light of Christian ideals the issues which are at stake, without either prejudice or heat, and to register his vote in accordance with his conscience under the most solemn sense of responsibility before GOD. He is bound, of course, to be a reformer, standing for cleanness of methods, probity of motives, honest thinking, class unselfishness, and the elimination of abuses and malpractices. He will tend in most cases to be a cross-bencher, in the sense of being independent of party caucuses and concerned only for social and political righteousness.

A Christian man who has leisure and opportunity can render enormous service by going into politics, more especially into municipal politics, which are too often surrendered to the tender mercies of corrupt, narrow-minded, or interested local wire-pullers. There is an enormous field of unselfish social service and opportunity lying open to Christian laymen in this connexion. There can be no truer form of work for the Church of GOD than the work of a municipal councillor who seeks not popularity but righteousness.

The carrying over of Christian ideals into national and international politics is equally indispensable. In the sphere of international affairs in particular, while other nations have, for the most part, rendered official lip-service from time to time to ideals of international morality, it has been reserved for Germany to declare openly for the repudiation of "sentiment," and for a policy of undisguised cynicism and real-politik. The doctrine that the state as such is exempt from moral obligation towards its neighbours, and that the whole political duty of man is exhausted in the service of his country and the promotion of her purely selfish interests and "will to power," has been exhibited in action by the Prussian Government in such a fashion as to incur the moral reprobation of the world. The cynical doctrines of real-politik, the belief that the "interests" of the state are in politics and diplomacy paramount, and that "the foreigner" is a natural enemy, the belief that in all international relationships selfish and self-interested considerations must really determine policy, are unfortunately by no means unrepresented, though they are not unchallenged, in the political life of other countries besides Germany. There are influential publicists in England to-day the principles of whose political thinking are really Prussian. It remains to be seen whether, when the time comes for peace to be made between the nations, the forces of international idealism will prove strong enough to carry the day, or whether we shall have a merely vindictive and "realist" peace which will contain within itself the seeds of future wars. There can be no question but that a Christian man is bound to stand both for the freedom of oppressed nationalities and for the right of all peoples freely to determine their own affairs, and also for the duty of nations as of individuals to love their neighbours as themselves, and to seek primarily not their own but each other's good. If these professions are to be more than nominal they must mean a readiness for national sacrifices and for national unselfishness in time of peace as in time of war.

Chapter IX

Christianity and War

Christianity is opposed to war, in the sense that if men and nations universally behaved as Christians, wars would cease. The ideal of the Kingdom of GOD involves the reign upon earth of universal peace. War is, therefore, in itself, an unchristian thing. It is, moreover, a barbarous and irrational method of determining disputes, since the factors which humanly speaking are decisive for success in war, viz. the organized and unflinching use of superior physical force, are in principle irrelevant to the rights or wrongs of the cause which may be at stake. The victories of might and right do not invariably coincide.

It is not surprising, therefore, that a certain proportion of Christians—the Quakers, for example, and many individuals who have either been influenced by the teaching of Tolstoy, or else, thinking the matter out for themselves, have arrived at similar conclusions to those of Tolstoy and the Quakers—should hold that in the event of war a man's loyalty to his earthly city must give way to his loyalty to his heavenly King in this matter. Experience shows that there are men who are prepared to suffer persecution, imprisonment, or death itself rather than violate their principles by service in the armed forces of the Crown.

There are obviously circumstances conceivable in which it would be the duty of all Christians to become "Conscientious Objectors." Such circumstances would arise in any case in which the state endeavoured to compel men's services in a war which their conscience disapproved. In the present European War it so happens that there are probably no Englishmen who regard the German cause as righteous and the Allies' cause as wrong. The problem of Conscientious Objection has, therefore, only arisen in the case of those Christians who hold the abstract doctrine of the absolute wrongness, in whatever circumstances, of all war as such.

There are those who, though personally rejecting this doctrine, consider that those who hold it are wrong only in that they are spiritually in advance of their time. The majority, however, of Christians have felt that the Pacifist or Quaker doctrine is not merely impracticable under present conditions, but that it rests upon a fallacious principle. For it appears to deny that physical force can ever be rightfully employed as the instrument of a moral purpose. In the last resort it is akin to the anti-sacramental doctrine which regards what is material as essentially opposed to what is spiritual.

The questions at issue are not really to be solved by the quotation of isolated texts or sayings of our Lord from the Gospels. What is really in dispute is the question of the form which, in the context of a given set of national and political circumstances, may rightfully be given to the application of the Christian principle of universal, righteous, and self-sacrificing Love. No one can dispute the fact that in certain circumstances Christianity may demand the readiness to die for others. Are there any circumstances in which Christianity may demand the readiness to slay for others, either personally, or mediately through service in a military machine which as a whole is the instrument of a national purpose only to be achieved through the slaughter of those in the ranks of the opposing armies?

The majority of Christians have answered this question in the affirmative. They have held that there are circumstances in which the claims of Love are more genuinely and adequately acknowledged by taking part in warfare than by abstaining from it. They have insisted that there are circumstances in which it is no true act of love, even towards the aggressor, or perhaps towards the aggressor least of all, to permit him to achieve an evil purpose unchecked: that resistance, even by force of arms, may be in the truest interests of the enemy himself. They have maintained that it is possible to fight in a Christian temper and spirit, without either personal malice or hatred of the foe: that not all killing is murder, and that to rob a man of physical life, as an incident in the assertion of the claims of righteousness, is not, from the point of view of those who believe in human immortality, to do him that ultimate and essential injury which it might otherwise be held to be.

No one, however, who has had anything to do with modern war can doubt that it is intrinsically beastly and devilish, or that it is apt to arouse passions, in all but the saintliest of men, which are of an extremely ugly kind. To affirm that it is possible, as a matter of theory, to fight in a wholly Christian spirit and temper, is not to assert that in actual practice more than a small minority of soldiers succeed in doing so. It is possible to be devoutly thankful that when the issue was posed by the conduct of the Germanic powers in the August of 1914 the British Empire replied by entering upon war, to hold that it was emphatically the right thing to do, and that it represented a course of conduct more intrinsically Christian than neutrality would have been. But it is not possible to maintain with truth that the British nation as a whole has been fighting either in a Christian temper or from Christian motives. It is undeniable that uglier motives and passions have crept in. Sermons in Christian pulpits upon such themes as the duty of forgiveness or the Christian ideal of love towards the enemy have been neither frequent nor popular. Undoubtedly the German Government in its general policy, and particular units of the German Army and Navy upon many occasions, have acted in such a way as to give provocation of the very strongest kind to the unregenerate human impulses of hatred and of revenge. It is not surprising, though it is regrettable, that under the influence of this provocation many persons, otherwise Christian, have either frankly abandoned the Christian doctrine of human brotherhood, or else have denied that the Germans are to be regarded as human beings. On the whole, and speaking very broadly, it may be said that the troops have shown themselves more Christian in these respects than have the civil population, though there are many exceptions upon both sides. It is to be feared that the Church, in so far as she has been represented by her clergy (though here, again, there are many exceptions), has been too anxious to be identified with a merely Jingo patriotism to exercise any very appreciable influence in restraint of unchristian passions. It is to be hoped and anticipated that there will be a strong reaction after the war both against militarism and the less desirable aspects of the military mind, and also against the belligerent temper and spirit—especially, perhaps, on the part of the men who have themselves served and suffered in the field.

Chapter X

Love, Courtship, and Marriage

No element in Christian practice has been more widely challenged in modern times than the Christian ideal of marriage. Our Lord's standard in these matters was simple and austere. "Whoso looketh on a woman to lust after her hath committed adultery already in his heart." "Whosoever shall put away his wife, saving for the cause of fornication" (the exceptive clause is of disputed authenticity) "causeth her to commit adultery: and whosoever shall marry her that is divorced committeth adultery."

The State in certain cases gives legal sanction to "adultery" in this latter sense, and there is a vocal and probably increasing demand that legal facilities for divorce upon various pretexts, with liberty of remarriage, shall be further extended. The Divorce Law Reform Union has announced its intention to promote in Parliament a Bill which, if carried, would have the effect of reducing legal marriage to a contract terminable after three years' voluntary separation by the will of either party. Doubtless a robust opposition will be offered by Christian people to the adoption of so lax a conception of marriage even by the State. Experience in other countries seems to show that unlimited facilities for divorce do not tend to the promotion either of happiness or of morals. But it needs to be recognized that the State, as such, is concerned only with the legal aspect of marriage as a civil contract, and that it has to legislate for citizens not all of whom profess Christian standards even in theory. The law of the State may well diverge from that of the Church with regard to this matter, though it does not follow that so lax a standard as that which is now proposed would be in the best interests even of the State.

The Church regards Christian marriage as indissoluble. In cases of adultery she counsels reconciliation, wherever possible, upon the basis of repentance on the part of the guilty and forgiveness on the part of the injured partner. If this is not possible the Church sanctions, if need so require, separation, but not remarriage. There are also unfortunately other cases in which the married relationship proves so intolerable as to render a temporary or permanent separation admissible as a last resort. The remarriage of either party during the lifetime of the other is nevertheless held to be unchristian. With the practical difficulties which beset the Church in the attempt to maintain within the circle of her own membership a stricter standard than that which is recognized by the Civil Law and by society at large we are not here concerned. Our concern is with the Christian standard as a positive ideal, on the effective maintenance of which, as Christians believe, depends the stability of the home and the Christian family, and the redemption of sex-relations from mere animalism and grossness.

A Christian husband takes his wife in matrimony "for better for worse, for richer for poorer, in sickness and in health, to love and to cherish, till death them do part, according to GOD'S holy ordinance." The step is irrevocable. The union is intended to be life-long. It has, moreover, in view not only "the mutual society, help, and comfort that the one ought to have of the other," but also "the procreation of children, to be brought up in the fear and nurture of the Lord, and to the praise of His holy Name." A few words may usefully be said under these heads.

(i) Marriage ought to be based upon love; and love, though naturally and normally involving the element of sexual attraction, ought to include also other and deeper elements. A Christian man who has lived a clean and disciplined life ought to be sufficiently master of his passions to avoid mistaking a merely temporary infatuation for such a genuine spiritual affinity as will survive the satisfaction of immediate desires and prove the stable basis of a life-companionship. Hasty marriages are a common and avoidable cause of subsequent unhappiness. It is obviously undesirable that couples should enter upon matrimony until there has been a sufficiently prolonged and intimate acquaintance to enable them to become reasonably sure both of themselves and of one another. In many cases there is much to be said for regarding betrothals in the first instance as provisional. It is better to break them off at the last moment than to marry the wrong person.

The Victorian conventions with regard to all these matters were thoroughly bad. Girls were brought up in carefully-guarded ignorance of the implications of matrimony and shielded by perpetual chaperonage from anything approaching comradeship with the opposite sex. Eventually they were in many cases stampeded into a marriage which had its origin either in a clandestine flirtation or in the designing operations of some match-making relative, who made it her business first to "throw the young people together" and then to suggest that they were virtually committed to one another by the mere fact of having met.

The reaction which has taken place against all this is upon the whole salutary. The new social tradition which is growing up makes it possible for the unmarried of both sexes to meet one another with comparative freedom, and to establish relations of friendship, which may subsequently ripen into love, unhampered by any such morbidly exciting atmosphere of intrigue and suggestion on the part of relatives and friends. But the new freedom of social intercourse, if it is not in its turn to prove disastrous, demands on the part of the young of both sexes a higher standard both of responsibility and self- control, and of knowledge of what is implied in the fact of sex. The experience of married life is, moreover, not likely to prove a success, save in rare instances, unless there is between the parties a real community of interests and tastes, unanimity, so far as may be, of ideals and of religious convictions, and at least no very great disparity of educational and intellectual equipment.

(ii) A Christian marriage includes among its purposes the procreation of children. It is here most of all that unanimity of ideal and of conviction between husband and wife is essential. A man and a woman ought not to take one another in marriage without first being assured of each other's mind upon this subject. "If marriage is to be a success each must learn respect for the other's personality, real give and take, and the horror of treating the other just as a means to his own pleasure, whether spiritual, intellectual, or physical: and both must think seriously of the responsibilities of parenthood. Husband and wife must work out their ideals together, in perfect frankness and sincerity, and it is impossible to have true and sacred ideals of their joint physical life unless there is the same openness and understanding and sympathy on this point as on all others."[17] There must be mutual consideration and self-control: the need for self-restraint and continence does not disappear with the entry upon marital relations: it is if anything intensified.

There is a real problem here which needs to be thought out. To the practice of "race-suicide," by which is meant the artificial restriction of parentage by the use of mechanical or other "preventives," Christian morality is violently opposed. On the other hand, it may reasonably be held that people ought not to bring children into the world in numbers which are wholly out of relation to their capacity to feed, clothe, educate, and train them. "The enormous families of which we hear in early Victorian times were not quite ideal for the mother or the children, nor for the father if he were not well off."[18] It may be found necessary in practice to limit the size of the family either upon economic grounds or (in particular instances) in the interest of the mother's health.

It is to be feared, however, that the modern tendency in both respects is to shirk the responsibilities of parenthood on grounds which are thoroughly selfish. The Victorian doctrine that "when GOD sends mouths He sends food to fill them" may have been

---

[17] Ideals of Home, by Gemma Bailey (National Mission Paper, No. 43).
[18] Ibid

unduly happy-go-lucky. The recent remark of an officer in a certain British regiment, that since he and his wife had only L8000 a year between them, he felt that he could not afford to have more than one child, was entirely shameless. It would seem, moreover, that the comparative childlessness of modern marriages is sometimes due not to the husband's reluctance, upon economic grounds, to beget children, but to the wife's reluctance to bear them, a reluctance which in some cases arises either from such shrinking from the physical pain and sacrifice of motherhood as goes beyond what is really justified, or from mere self-indulgent absorption in social pursuits and pleasures. There ought to be in a Christian marriage more of the true spirit of adventure and romance, a greater readiness for sacrifice, a more willing acceptance of parental responsibilities, and of the obligation of self-denial for the children's sake. There can be no question but that modern families— with the paradoxical exception of the families of the very poor—have been tending to be smaller than they either need be or ought to be.

At the same time it is generally conceded that some measure of limitation is in most cases reasonable and necessary. The vitally important thing is that such necessary and reasonable limitation should be secured not by artificial evasion of the consequences of intercourse, but by self-control and deliberate temporary abstinence at certain periods from the intercourse of sex. [19]

For the union of the sexes in marriage is according to the mind of the Christian Church an essentially pure and holy thing. It is a sacrament of the fusion of two personalities, whereby they are at once individually and mutually enriched, and at the same time mystically and spiritually knit together in such a way as to become in the sight of GOD indissolubly one: the unity of husband and wife being comparable, according to a famous saying of S. Paul, to the unity which exists between Christ and His Church. Now, although, from this point of view, the significance

---

[19] It may be suggested that in cases of genuine perplexity it is advisable to consult, as occasion may require, either a medical man who is also a Christian, or a wise—and preferably a married—spiritual guide.

of married life is to a great extent impoverished and frustrated, if intercourse is so regulated as to render the marriage childless not in fact merely, but in intention, yet it does not follow that procreation must be directly in view on every individual occasion, since the mystical value of intercourse as a spiritual sacrament of love may still exist in independence of such intention. It is nevertheless, surely, clear that a Christian man and his wife are morally precluded from coming together except with a deep sense of the sacredness of what they do and of its intimate connexion with the mysteries of life and birth, and a corresponding readiness, in the event of conception taking place, to accept the ensuing responsibility for the child as a sacred trust from GOD, "the Father from whom all fatherhood in heaven and on earth is named." With the use of "preventives" and other devices, which degrade into a mere means of carnal satisfaction an act which is meant to bear a deeply spiritual and religious meaning, the Christian interpretation of marriage seems plainly and obviously incompatible.

A few words may be added with regard to the upbringing and education of children. Here, again, there has been a reaction—which upon the whole is good—from the unduly rigorous disciplinary methods of the past. It may be doubted, however, whether the reaction has not in some cases been carried too far. Children ought to be controlled and disciplined by their parents, and no expenditure of care and thought and tact is too great to devote to the rightful training of their characters. But experience seems to show that parents sometimes fail to recognize that their children grow up. It is important that in proportion as they grow towards maturity of character and independence of personality the strictness of parental discipline should be gradually relaxed. At a certain stage the real influence of parents upon their children will depend upon their refusal to assert direct authority. Not a few of the minor tragedies of home life arise from the ill-judged action of parents who treat as children sons and daughters who are virtually grown up.

The problem of the religious education of children cannot here be discussed in detail, but three or four leading principles may be suggested.

(1) It ought not to be necessary to say that children should not be taught to regard as true statements or doctrines which their parents believe to be in fact false. This applies in particular to certain views of the Bible. The ideal should be so to teach the child that in later life he may have nothing to unlearn.

(2) When children are old enough to read they should be encouraged to read the Gospels. They ought not, however, to read the Old Testament, with the exception of certain Psalms and other specially selected passages, until they are of an age to distinguish what is Christian from what is Jewish, and to recognize the principle of religious development.

(3) Children should be taught in the first instance the practice rather than the theory of religion: devotions in which doctrine is implicit, rather than doctrine as such. As their minds expand they will ask the reasons for what they do and the meaning of the worship in which they engage, and they will need to have suggested to them an elementary, but not a stereotyped, theology. They should from the beginning be encouraged to think and question freely on religious subjects.

(4) They should occasionally accompany their parents to Church, and in particular should from time to time be present when the latter receive Holy Communion. They should have the service explained to them in a simple fashion, and should be encouraged to look forward to the time when they will be confirmed, and become communicants themselves.

Part III

The Maintenance of the Christian Life

Chapter I

How to Begin

The practice of Christianity depends for its possibility upon the existence and maintenance within the soul of an inward principle of spiritual life towards GOD. The reason why so many nominal Christians fail conspicuously to manifest the fruits of Christianity in their lives is simply that they have no vital personal experience of the power and efficacy of the life in Christ. They have never been effectually gripped by the religion which they nominally profess. They are not transformed, or in process of being transformed, by the Holy Spirit's power.

The plain man, confronted by the Christian ideal, if he does not at once dismiss it as impracticable, is apt to ask, or at least to wonder, how he is to begin. It is a question to which no cut-and-dried answer can be given. But at least no beginning is likely to lead to very much in the way of fulfilment which does not sooner or later involve something like personal "conversion" of heart. Conversions may be sudden, or they may be gradual: but religion, if it is to be a reality, means in the end the establishment of vital personal relations with the living Christ. It means the acceptance of His challenge, self-surrender to His appeal, the combination of an acknowledged desire to serve Him with acknowledged impotence and bankruptcy before GOD.

Sooner or later the Spirit convinces men of sin. Either a man, essaying light-heartedly to follow Christ, discovers in the very attempt his inability to do so, and is found traitor to his Master's cause in the first encounter: or else, it may be, at the very outset, the consciousness of what has been wrong in conduct and character and motive in the past stands as a damning record between his soul and GOD, and forbids him without repentance

118

to take service in the campaign of Christ at all. The consciousness of sin as a "horrid impediment" in the soul is not, of course, true penitence until a man has been brought to realize in the light of the Cross that the difference between what he is and what he might have been is treachery to Him whose man (in virtue of his baptism) he was meant to be, and that by being what he is, and acting as he has acted, he has consciously or unconsciously contributed to the wounds wherewith Eternal Love is wounded in the house of His friends.

The measure of a man's penitence, whether early or late developed in him, is very apt to be the measure of his spiritual insight and of his spiritual sincerity. The familiar words of the hymn—

"They who fain would serve Thee best

Are conscious most of wrong within,"

are profoundly true to Christian experience. But repentance—which is sorrow for sin in the light of the Cross—is abortive and merely results in spiritual paralysis unless it issues in confession—that is, frank and open acknowledgment before GOD, and if need be also before His Church—and the seeking and finding of reconciliation and forgiveness as the unmerited gift of GOD in Christ.

There are those in whose case the inward conviction of sin and the realization of the need for pardon are the first impulses of awakening spiritual life. There are others with whom it is not so. They are conscious of the attractiveness of the Man Christ Jesus. They would desire to be on His side and to be of the number of His disciples. They are dimly aware, or at least they more than half suspect, that in Him is to be found the satisfaction of a need for which their soul cries out. With S. Peter they find themselves saying to Christ, "Lord, to whom shall we go? Thou hast the words of eternal life," But they cannot as yet with any inward reality profess themselves conscience- stricken with regard to the past. They are not aware of themselves as conspicuous sinners, or indeed, it may be, as sinners at all. The experience of penitence and of Divine forgiveness must come to them, if it is to come at all, at a later stage. It is not by that postern that they enter upon the Way of the Spirit.

But the Way is in either case the way of fellowship, and the Spirit is the spirit of discipline. The newly found spiritual life, however awakened, needs to be maintained and fostered by fellowship in the Church, by regular habits of Christian devotion, by faithful communion in the Sacrament of Life. Plainly, if a man is not already confirmed, his first step must be to be prepared for confirmation: if he has been confirmed, but has lapsed from communion, he must resume the communicant life. He needs to claim the status and privilege of effective membership in the Body of Christ, and to form for himself a rule of inward life and discipline. Rules of devotional life must necessarily vary in accordance with a man's surroundings and opportunities, and perhaps in some of their details in accordance with a man's temperament. But at least there ought to be a rule of regular private prayer, a rule of regular communion, a rule of Bible-reading or "meditation," and a rule of self-denial and orderliness in daily personal life.

Chapter II

Prayer

Prayer is a difficult matter, both in theory and in practice. But it is essential to learn to pray.

It is important to recognize that the scope of Christian prayer is much wider than mere intercession or petition. It is the communion of the soul with GOD, and its purpose is union with the life of GOD in identity of purpose with His will. The beginning of prayer is a sursum corda, a lifting up of the heart to GOD. It is well to remember that true prayer is never a solitary act, even when a man prays in solitude. We pray not as individuals but as members of a Family, and our prayer is spiritually united and knit together with the common prayer-life of the universal Church, of which it forms a part. We pray, moreover, not to wrest to our private ends the purposes of GOD, not to induce Him, so to speak, to do our wills instead of His, but to unite our wills with His will, as children who have confidence in their Father. True prayer is offered in the Name of Christ—that is, it is prayed in His Spirit, according to His mind and will. It can never, therefore, be selfish or self-centred. The Lord's Prayer is its model and its type. A few words may be said in explanation of this prayer.

It begins with a recognition of the common Fatherhood of GOD. It is only as members of His Family that we can approach Him: He is in no sense our personal or private GOD, but the common Father of us all.

And our Father is "in heaven"—that is, supreme, eternal, the Lord and Ruler of all things. His Name is holy, and to be hallowed: it is in reverence and deepest worship that we bow before Him. He is King, and we pray that His Kingship may be realized, in earth as it is in heaven: and that His will may be done—that is the supreme desire of our hearts, and the highest object of our petitions.

And therefore we are vowed to His service: and because we are sure that He will supply whatever we really need to that end, we pray in confidence for daily needs both spiritual and bodily—"Give us this day our daily bread." And remembering that we are unprofitable and faithless and disloyal servants we ask forgiveness for our sins, well knowing that we can only be forgiven as we ourselves are ready to forgive. And so looking to the future and mindful of our frailty we pray that GOD will not lead us into "temptation" or trial, without at the same time providing a way of deliverance from the assaults of evil. The prayer customarily ends with an ascription of praise and glory to GOD.

That is the type and model of Christian prayer: and prayer is truly Christian just in so far as the spirit and temper of the Lord's Prayer inspires it. We can only pray rightly in the Holy Spirit. "We know not what to pray for as we ought: but the Spirit helpeth our infirmities."

As for the technique of prayer, a man, on kneeling or standing to pray, will do well to spend a short time first in silence and recollection, waiting in stillness upon GOD, remembering His presence, His holiness, His love, and His responsiveness to His children's cry. Let him next make an act of adoration, spoken or unspoken, and invoke GOD the Holy Spirit to enable him to pray aright. Then let him pour out before GOD all that is in his heart, his troubles, his anxieties, his perplexities, his sins: let him ask for forgiveness: let him give thanks: let him pray for the coming of GOD'S Kingdom, in its various aspects: commending to GOD'S guidance and protection all right causes and aspirations in the world, in things both social and political and international, in things ecclesiastical, in things moral and religious and missionary: let him add personal and private intercessions for those near and dear to him and for those whom he meets in the daily intercourse of life: and let him end as he began, in a few moments of quiet waiting upon GOD.

That is the general scheme of a Christian's private prayers. They should include in due proportion the several elements of adoration, thanksgiving, penitence, petition, and intercession.

They need not be lengthy. "Use not vain repetitions, as the heathen do: for they think that they shall be heard for their much speaking." It is quality and not quantity of prayer that counts. And the prayers of a busy man must necessarily be short.

But it is worth while taking time and trouble over the ordering of one's prayers. A man's intercessions, in particular, are not likely in practice to have the width, the range, and the variety which are desirable, unless they are planned and ordered in accordance with a coherent scheme which is thought out in advance. It is the part of wisdom to keep a note-book, in which names and subjects for intercessory prayer may be jotted down and distributed over the days of the week for use in due rotation. Such schemes, however, if drawn up and used, should be revised from time to time, and not suffered to become a mechanical burden or a legal bondage. There should be freedom and spontaneity in a Christian's prayers. It is well to have rules, and to try not to be prevented by mere slackness from keeping them. But it is important to see to it that the self-imposed rule is so framed as to prove genuinely conducive to reality in prayer, and suitably adapted to opportunity and circumstance: and it is very often a good thing from time to time, in the interests of freedom, quite deliberately to break one's rules.

With regard to forms and methods of prayer, it is desirable that men should learn to pray freely in their own words, or even in no words at all. Provided a man remembers reverence, he need not stand on ceremony with GOD. But it is advisable also to use books and manuals of prayer —at any rate in the first instance: to use them, but not to be tied to them. Many such manuals have been compiled and published within recent years: the majority of them are unsatisfactory in varying degrees. A few, however, can confidently be recommended: especially Prayers for the City of God, compiled by G. C. Binyon (Longmans); Prayers for Common Use (Universities Mission to Central Africa, Dartmouth St., Westminster); and Sursum Corda, a Handbook of Intercession and Thanksgiving, arranged by W. H. Frere and A. L. Illingworth (A. E. Mowbray and Co., Ltd.).

Prayer need not be confined to stated hours and times. Interpreting prayer at its widest, the ideal should be to "pray without ceasing." It was said of an early Christian writer that his life was "one continuous prayer": and it is well to form the habit of inwardly lifting up the heart to GOD from time to time in the midst of daily cares and business. Where Churches are kept open it is often possible in passing to spare time to enter and kneel for two or three minutes in quiet and recollection before GOD: but it is perfectly possible to pray inwardly at any time and in any environment. Fixed times of prayer, nevertheless, there must also be: and a man should at least pray in the morning upon rising and in the evening before going to bed. If a time can also be secured for midday prayer, so much the better: but this is more difficult. To have formed a really fixed and stable habit of daily prayer is an enormous step forwards in Christian life. Much depends upon learning to rise regularly at a fixed hour before breakfast: and this in turn depends upon a regularity in going to bed, which under modern conditions of life it is not always easy to achieve. If a man is obliged to be up so late at night that it is morally certain that he will be too tired to pray with much reality before turning in, he should endeavour, if it is at all possible, to secure some time for prayer at an earlier stage in the evening.

Difficulties in the life of prayer beset everybody. Thoughts have a way of wandering, the "saying" of prayers tends to become mechanical, moods vary, and there are times in most men's lives when they feel it almost impossible to pray with any sense of reality. A man should not lightly be discouraged. He may be recommended to remind himself that GOD knows all about it, and that the resolute offering of his will to GOD at such times, in defiance of distraction and difficulty, has special value. It is well to take God into one's confidence. "If GOD bores you, tell Him that He does." He is no exacting tyrant, but a Father caring for His sons. Those who care to do so may find Prayer and some of its Difficulties, by the Rev. W. J. Carey (Mowbray & Co.), a helpful book to read in this connexion.

A final word may be said with regard to a theoretical difficulty which many people feel in connexion with the intercessory and petitionary sides of prayer. Since GOD'S will, it may be argued, is presumably going to be done in any case, and since He knows the real needs both of ourselves and of our friends better than we do, what is the point of praying for them? To many people it may be a sufficient practical answer to refer to the example and precept of Christ, who both taught and practised intercessory prayer. But it is possible to go a little further, and to point out that it appears to be GOD'S will, not merely that such and such a thing should be done, but that it should be done in response to our human prayers. True it is that "your Father knoweth what things ye have need of, before ye ask Him": but our Lord emphasized this truth, not as a round for regarding prayer as futile or unnecessary, but as a reason for praying. For prayer is an expression of the filial spirit towards our Father, and the more simply and naturally we approach GOD as children, making our petitions before Him with childlike hearts, the more truly will our prayers be in accordance with that spirit of sonship which is the mind of Christ. At the same time, the knowledge that our Father is wiser as well as greater than we will forbid us to clamour for what in wisdom is denied us, and will in general govern the spirit and scope of our petitions. Just as our Lord points out that an earthly father, if asked for bread, will not give his child a stone, so conversely in the experience of every Christian it often happens that in his blindness he asks a stone, and is given bread. But no Christian will ask deliberately and knowingly for stones.

Chapter III

Self-Examination and Repentance

"The unexamined life," said Plato, "is not worth living." Similar advice was given by Marcus Aurelius. The practice of self-examination, therefore, is not distinctive of Christianity: it is an obvious dictate of wisdom, wherever life and conduct are regarded seriously, that a man should from time to time take stock of himself in the light of his ideals and learn to know and recognize in detail where and how he has fallen short, and what are the besetting sins and weaknesses against which he must contend.

The Christian man will judge and try his life by the standards of Christ, with growing sensitiveness of conscience as spiritual experience deepens: not shrinking from the confession of sin and failure, desiring not to be self-deceived, but to know and to acknowledge the truth. There is nothing in this of priggishness or unreality. It is a necessary discipline. The Christian life is meant to bear the fruit of a character developing in growing likeness to the character of Christ: but none is suddenly made perfect: the old Adam dies hard: and the Christian by confession of repeated failure may at least learn the lesson of humility and self-distrust.

The rightful complement of self-distrust is trust in GOD: the rightful issue of self-examination and confession is the realization of divine forgiveness, fresh courage, and a new start. The very core of the Gospel is here. He who has bidden men forgive those who trespass against them "unto seventy times seven" is not to be outdone in generosity by man. But in order that sin may be forgiven it must be acknowledged as sin against GOD and treachery to Christ, and repented of with true sorrow of heart. Repentance is not mere self-contempt, self-pity, or remorse. It is sorrow for sin, which has for its motive the love of GOD and the realization that human sin meant and means in the experience of GOD the Cross.

Nothing so deepens the religious life as true repentance, nor is there anything so fatal to true religion as self-righteousness. "If we say that we have no sin, we deceive ourselves, and the truth is not in us." "To whom little is forgiven, the same loveth little." But the first prerequisite of repentance is self-knowledge—a difficult matter. Gross carnal offences, strong and flagrant sins, if such there be, are obvious and upon the surface. The subtler sins of the spirit— thoughtlessness, for example, or snobbishness or priggishness and pride—though we are quick to remark upon them in others, are apt in our own case to pass undetected. It is the Spirit who convinces men of sin. Only as we are resolute to enter into "the mind of the Spirit" can we hope to know ourselves as in the sight of GOD we really are.

The matter is complicated by the fact that those who, as things are, most systematically practise self-examination and confession of sin too often view the matter in a somewhat narrowly ecclesiastical spirit, and make use of forms of self-examination which mix up real and serious moral offences with "sins" which are merely ceremonial, trivial, or imaginary, as though the two stood precisely upon the same level. "One must abstain from sexual sin and not go to dissenting places of worship; one must not steal and must be sure to abstain from meat on Fridays." A man's own sense of reality should enable him to guard against this sort of thing, and if fixed forms of self-examination are used, to use them with discretion.

The forms most commonly suggested in manuals of devotion are based upon the Ten Commandments. This is in accordance with the teaching of the compilers of the English Prayer-book, who, after bidding intending communicants to "search and examine" their "own consciences (and that not lightly, and after the manner of dissemblers with GOD)," proceed to lay down that "the way and means thereto is: First, to examine your lives and conversations by the rule of God's commandments: and whereinsoever ye shall perceive yourselves to have offended, either by will, word or deed, there to bewail your own sinfulness, and to confess yourselves to Almighty GOD, with full purpose of amendment of life."

The Commandments are, however, as they stand, both negative in form and Judaistic in character, and if used in this way as a "rule" of Christian conduct must be spiritualized and reinterpreted in the light of the Gospel. The second and fourth Commandments, in particular, are in their literal significance obsolete for Christians: it is a false Puritanism which would forbid sculpture and religious symbolism in the adornment of a Christian church, nor is any one in the modern world likely to confuse the symbol with the thing symbolized: while the observance of the Sabbath is part of that older ceremonial "law" from which S. Paul insisted that Christian converts should be free (Coloss. ii. 16). There is, however, a spiritual idolatry which consists in allowing any other object than the glory of GOD and the doing of His will to have the primary place in the determination of conduct—there are men who worship money, or comfort, or ambition, or their own domestic happiness, or even themselves. And the Commandment about the Sabbath, though it has no literal value to-day (and certainly no direct bearing upon the sanction or significance of Sunday) may serve to suggest the important principle that a man is responsible before GOD for the use he makes of his time, and that it is a religious duty (not confined to any particular day of the week) to distribute it in due proportion, according to circumstance and opportunity, with proper regard to the rightful claims of work, of worship, and of recreation and rest. The remaining Commandments are capable of being similarly interpreted as suggesting broad positive principles rather than as merely prohibiting wrong actions of a particular and definite kind: and so treated they form as convenient a framework as any other for a scheme of questions for self-examination.

It is possible, however, that some men may prefer to use as their basis some standard more distinctively Christian than the ancient law of Judaism—for example, the Beatitudes (Matt. v. 1-12) or the "fruits of the Spirit" (Gal. v. 22). A man will in any case do well either to frame or to adapt his own scheme for self-examination, with special regard paid to whatever he may discover by experience to be a besetting sin or weakness, or a temptation to which he is particularly exposed. It should be remembered that the measure of what is wrong in a man's life is the measure of the contrast between his character and that of Christ, and that the chief flaws in Christian character and achievement (which are also those most likely to pass undetected) are not uncommonly such as fall under the head of "sins of omission" rather than of commission—the leaving undone of what ought to have been done, the failure to exhibit positively in relation to GOD and man the qualities of faith and hope and love. A man should ask himself wherein he has chiefly failed, and come short of the glory of GOD: whether he is loyally observing any self-imposed rule of life and discipline, and fulfilling any resolutions which may have been made, or any obligations which have been undertaken. Having made in this manner an honest attempt to discover his own shortcomings and failures before GOD, let him with equal honesty confess them, seek forgiveness, and in the spirit of repentance and restored sonship start again.

The late Lieutenant Donald Hankey, better known as "A Student in Arms," criticizes Churchmen of a certain type as being unwholesomely preoccupied with the thought of their sins, and allowing their consciences to become a burden to them. They should, he says, 'think less of themselves, and trust the Holy Spirit more. The advice is excellent: but morbid scrupulosity is not a common fault of English laymen. The habit, as Mr. Chesterton expresses it, of "chopping up life into small sins with a hatchet" is, of course, to be avoided: but the purpose of self-examination and self-knowledge is not to encourage morbid introspection, but by frank acknowledgment and repentance to get rid of the past and with recovered hope and serenity to reach forward towards the future. A man cannot "walk in the Spirit" unless he is inwardly "right with GOD."

With regard to sacramental confession, the rule of the Church of England is sane and clear. It may be expressed by saying that "none must, but all may, and some should" make use of it. In the case of a conscience seriously burdened in such a way that a man hesitates to present himself for Holy Communion unabsolved, to go to confession is obviously the right remedy. There are other cases in which men find by experience that it helps them to be more honest and candid with themselves, with GOD, and with the Church, if they go to confession from time to time as a piece of self-discipline and a needed spiritual tonic. Yet others discover that they flounder less in spiritual things, and that their religious life is deepened and made stronger, if they place themselves for a time under wise direction. Systematic direction, of course, has obvious dangers. It may tend to destroy independence of character. It may cause a man to become "priest-ridden." But the dangers are not inevitable, and there are without doubt cases in which it is of value. Much obviously depends upon the wisdom and common sense of the director. The Prayer-book refers penitents to a "discreet and learned" minister of GOD'S Word. If a man proposes to practise habitual confession he will do well to assure himself of the discretion and learning of the priest whose help he seeks.

The method of making a sacramental confession is simple. Self- examination is made beforehand, the results being, if need be, written down, either in full, or in the form of notes to assist the memory. A first confession should cover the whole life so far as remembered, from childhood upwards: subsequent confessions the period since the last was made. The confession should aim at completeness, an effort being made to remember not only specific acts of wrongdoing, but slight failings and weaknesses of character and the general lines and tendencies of faulty spiritual development. Symptoms should, if possible, be distinguished from causes, habits and tendencies and besetting sins from isolated acts. Cases in which a sin has been deliberate should be noted as such: but there should be no dwelling upon extenuating circumstances or intermingling of claims to virtues or graces of character with the admission of defects. No names may be mentioned, nor may third persons be incriminated by any form of words which would enable the confessor to recognize their identity. The priest hears the confession sitting in a chair. The penitent kneels beside him and confesses as follows:—"I confess to GOD Almighty, the Father, the Son and the Holy Ghost, before the whole company of heaven, and before you, that I have sinned in thought, word, and deed, by my own fault. Especially I accuse myself that (since my last confession, which was...ago) I have committed the following sins.... [Here follows the confession in detail: after which]. ... For these and all my other sins which I cannot now remember, I humbly ask pardon of GOD, and of you, father, penance, counsel and absolution. Wherefore I ask GOD to have mercy upon me, and you to pray for me to the Lord our GOD. Amen."

The confessor then gives advice and counsel according to his wisdom, commonly imposes a penance, and if assured of the sincerity of the penitent, pronounces absolution according to the form prescribed in the Prayer-book Office for the Visitation of the Sick.

Chapter IV

Corporate Worship and Communion

The really essential thing is the Communion. There may be minor outward differences as to the manner of its celebration: you shall find in one parish a tradition of Puritan bareness, in another a full and rich ceremonial symbolism, with lights and vestments. A man may have his personal preferences, but it is a mistake to attach undue importance either to the presence or to the absence of the external adjuncts of worship. What matters is the Body and Blood of Christ.

A man must have his own regular rule with regard to Communion. To communicate spasmodically or upon impulse at irregular intervals is not the way to build up a stable Christian character. Where circumstances make possible the leading of a fairly regular life and give adequate opportunity for preparation beforehand, weekly communion is the best rule. Where this is not possible, a fortnightly or even a monthly rule may in particular cases be the best.

Preparation for Communion should be real, but need not be elaborate. It should be made overnight, and should include a review of the period since the last Communion was made, prayers for pardon and new resolves, if possible a short meditation on the essential meaning of the Sacrament, and the selection of some particular theme to be the focus of intercession at the service itself.

At the actual service it is well to arrive early, with a few moments to spare for quiet and recollected prayer before the Liturgy begins. The first part of the service is preparatory. Any pauses or intervals should be filled up by private prayers.[20] From the moment of consecration until the end of the service the mind should be concentrated as far as possible upon the thought of Christ's realized Presence. A man should go up to the altar to receive Communion as one desiring to meet his Lord and to be

---

[20] Forms and suggestions which, may be used by those who find them helpful are provided for this purpose in any manual of devotion.

renewed in Him, returning subsequently to his place to render thanks for so great a Gift. When the service is over it is best not to hurry out of church, but to linger for further thanksgiving and prayer as occasion serves.

It is an ancient rule or custom of the Church to receive Holy Communion fasting, giving precedence to the food of the soul over that of the body. To insist rigidly upon such a rule in any and every set of circumstances is a piece of unintelligent and unchristian legalism: but many persons are of opinion that to observe it wherever it is reasonably possible to do so makes for reality. There is a real value in the element of asceticism and self-discipline involved in the effort to rise early and come fasting to church: and the fast may be interpreted as a kind of outward sacrament of the inward reality of spiritual preparation—a preparation of the body corresponding to the preparation of the soul, It is, moreover, an advantage of the early morning hour that the mind is undistracted by the occupations and diversions of the day. For all these reasons the early morning Communion is to be preferred to Communion at a later hour.

Whether a man is a weekly communicant or not, he should in any case be present as a worshipper at Holy Communion Sunday by Sunday, and should regard attendance at the weekly Eucharist as the most essential part of church-going. No one who makes it a rule of his life to be present on Sundays and other festivals of the Church at Holy Communion ever has cause to regret having done so.

A man who for any reason (_e.g. by the nature of his employment) is debarred from attending regularly on Sundays should, if possible, secure an opportunity of regular attendance at Holy Communion on a week-day. There are usually churches to be found, at least in the towns, which have an early morning Eucharist daily throughout the week: and advantage can also be taken of this if on any particular occasion the regular Sunday Communion has been missed. If neither Sunday nor week-day opportunities are available, the need should be met by what is known as "spiritual communion": that is to say, a man should read over the Liturgy in private, unite himself in spirit with the Eucharist as celebrated in the particular church with which he happens to be most familiar (as representing for him the worship of the Church Universal), and pray that he may receive the spiritual benefits of Communion though deprived for the time being of the actual Sacrament. Apart from the "early service," which is now almost universal, schemes of worship upon Sunday mornings vary in different parishes. In some churches Matins and Litany are sung and a sermon preached, a late Eucharist without music being commonly celebrated about noon: in other parishes Matins is said quietly without music at a comparatively early hour, and the Eucharist is solemnly sung, with a sermon, as the principal service of the forenoon, usually without more than a very limited number of communicants, partly because if the bulk of the congregation communicate at a sung Eucharist the service becomes intolerably long, and partly because the majority of those desiring to receive Communion have done so fasting at an earlier hour.

In large towns a man can usually find churches of either type according to his preference. In "single-church areas" he ought for the sake of fellowship and good example to conform, as a rule, to what is customary. It is desirable, in a general way, to be identified with the corporate worship of the parish: but it is worth remarking that, apart from the weight due to this general consideration, there is no particular sacredness about the hour of eleven o'clock, and a man who has communicated before breakfast, and perhaps contemplates attendance, later on, at Evensong, may not unreasonably feel justified in devoting the forenoon of Sunday (which is usually his solitary morning's leisure in the week) to other purposes than those of worship. If the preacher is worth listening to (which is not invariably the case) it is a good thing to go and hear him: and it is well, therefore, to attend one or other of the services (morning or evening) at which a sermon is preached. But it is not essential to attend both: and the question may be raised whether one sermon a Sunday is not as much as most men can profitably digest. A sermon is in any case (except at the Eucharist) a detachable appendix to a Church service; and it is both possible and legitimate either to attend the service and leave the church before the sermon, or to avoid the service and come in time to hear the sermon, according to preference or opportunity.

As regards external details of observance, kneeling, and not squatting, should be the attitude adopted for prayer. It is customary to turn eastwards for the Creed, and in some churches, though not in others, to kneel at the reference to the Incarnation in the course of the Nicene Creed. It is also a common practice in some churches to genuflect (_i.e. to drop for a moment upon one knee) on rising from one's place to go up to the altar to communicate, in reverence for the Blessed Sacrament. A man should adapt his personal usage in these minor details to whatever appears to be customary in the particular church in which he is worshipping.

It is often extremely difficult for the clergy to know personally the men of their congregations, since it is rare in most neighbourhoods for the men to be at home during the hours when it is possible for the clergy to visit. In these circumstances a man ought to be willing to take the initiative in making himself known to the clergy of his parish, and to co-operate as far as possible in any effort which may be made, through parochial Church Councils or otherwise, to develop the spirit of fellowship in a congregation. There is very often about Anglican Church worship a stiffness and frigidity which badly needs to be broken down. Appropriated seats, where they exist, are a particular curse, and anything which can be done in the way of abandoning chosen seats, even if "bought and paid for," to strangers in the interests of charity is a real piece of Christian service. A stranger ought not to be made to feel uncomfortable, but to be welcomed in every possible way. The ideal is that every church, in every part of it, should be free and open at all times to all comers.

Chapter V

The Devotional Use of the Bible

It is to be feared that the habit of reading the Bible in private for purposes of devotion has largely dropped out of modern usage, partly by reason of the general stress and urgency of modern life, and partly because men do not quite know what to make of the Bible when they read it. They are aware of the existence of what are called "critical questions," but they do not know precisely the kind of differences which criticism has made. It is a pity to acquiesce in an attitude of this kind, and it is greatly to be desired that the habit of reading the Bible regularly and becoming familiar with its contents should be revived.

There are two distinct methods of reading the Bible which are of value. One is to take a particular book and to read it straight through like a novel, in order to get the impression of the writer's message as a whole. Advantage may be taken of occasional opportunities of Sunday or week-day leisure for this purpose. If the book is studied with the help of a good commentary, so much the better. A man who would be ashamed to be wholly unfamiliar with modern or classical literature ought to be equally ashamed to be wholly unfamiliar with the literature of the Hebrews.

The second method of reading the Bible consists in the devotional study of particular passages, sometimes called by the formidable name of "meditation." The parts of the Bible best adapted for this purpose are the Gospels, certain portions of the Epistles, many of the Psalms, and portions of the greater Prophets. The essence of the method is to read over a short passage quietly after prayer for spiritual guidance, to browse over it for a few minutes and follow out any train of thought which may be suggested by it, to apply its message in whatever way may seem most real and practical to the spiritual problems of immediate daily life, and to conclude with prayer and resolution for the future. It is not practicable for the majority of men to make such a "meditation" a matter of daily habit, though this may easily be possible for people of leisure. But it may be suggested that it is both practicable and abundantly worth while for ordinary people to allot at least half an hour a week for such a purpose. Our fathers unquestionably fed and nurtured their souls to an extraordinary degree by spiritual reading. It ought to be possible for modern people, in spite of modern distractions, to acquire and maintain the capacity to do the same.

Chapter VI

Almsgiving and Fasting

The two things were originally closely connected. Men fasted in order to give to others the savings which resulted from a reduced expenditure on personal needs. "Lent savings" represent a modern revival of this idea. The essence of Christian almsgiving is that it should be the expression of Christian charity or love: and love means the willingness to serve others, at cost to self. Gifts and subscriptions which represent merely the largess of a man's superfluity and cost nothing in the way of personal self-denial are not really in this sense almsgiving. The Gospel prefers the widow's mite to the rich man's large but not really generous contribution, in cases where the larger sum represents the lesser personal cost.

It was the rule of the ancient Jewish Law that a man should give away a tenth part of what he possessed, but this ought not to be adopted under modern conditions as a literal precept. The poor cannot afford to spare so large a fraction of their incomes. The wealthy can in many cases give away a much larger proportion without feeling particularly stinted. It is the duty of every man whose income is above the line of actual poverty (_i.e. exceeds what is necessary for the literal subsistence in food, shelter, and clothing of himself and those dependent upon him for support) to consider with his own conscience before GOD what proportion should be set aside for educational and other purposes, and what proportion should be directly given away in charity. Anonymous subscriptions are the best, and the amount available for distribution should be carefully allocated as between rival claims. Details, of course, must vary: but a certain proportion should in any case be given for the purposes of directly religious work at home and abroad. A man who really believes in the universality of the Gospel will in particular subscribe to the full extent of his capacity to foreign missions.

With regard to fasting it has been suggested in an earlier chapter of this book that there should be some personal rule of self-denial in a man's life. A table of fasts and days of abstinence is printed in the Prayer-book, though the Church of England does not normally prescribe in detail how such days are to be observed. It is worth remarking that the spirit is not necessarily in contradiction to the letter; but meticulous outward observances are not of the essence of Christianity, nor is it desirable to obtrude such observances in an ostentatious manner in mixed society. The rule of the Gospel with regard both to almsgiving and to fasting is that such things should be done in secret. It is usual, however, for Church people, at least in normal circumstances, to pay some special regard to the observance of Lent, and particularly of Holy Week, as a season of fasting and self-denial, and also (with a less degree of strictness) to the four weeks of Advent as leading up to Christmas. It is a good thing to enter into the observance of these and other seasons of the Christian year so far as circumstances permit: and at the least to make a point, if it is at all possible, of reading during Lent and Advent a more or less serious book of a religious or theological kind, or in other ways endeavouring to deepen, by some special practice or observance, the inward devotional life. The Sunday Collects, Epistles, and Gospels are of course appointed with special reference to the significance of the various seasons in the Church's year, and provide suitable passages for private meditation at such times. Advantage may also be taken of the special courses of sermons and additional services provided in almost every parish during the seasons of Lent and Advent. Loyalty to the Brotherhood in matters even of minor observance is a great principle to be borne in mind in this connexion. There is usually a method in the Church's madness, and her prescriptions and counsels are the product of a very considerable empirical acquaintance with the workings of the human soul.

The End

139

www.ingramcontent.com/pod-product-compliance
Lightning Source LLC
Chambersburg PA
CBHW071810090426
42737CB00012B/2027